D1236521

WOMAN – NATION – STATE

Woman – Nation – State

Edited by

Nira Yuval-Davis

Senior Lecturer in Sociology
Thames Polytechnic

and

Floya Anthias

Senior Lecturer in Sociology
Thames Polytechnic

Consultant Editor
Jo Campling

MACMILLAN

First published 1989

Published by
THE MACMILLAN PRESS LTD
Houndmills, Basingstoke, Hampshire RG21 2XS
and London
Companies and representatives
throughout the world

Typeset by Goodfellow & Egan Ltd, Cambridge
Printed and bound in Great Britain at
The Camelot Press Ltd, Southampton

British Library Cataloguing in Publication Data
Women, nation, state.
   1. Society. Role of women. Political aspects
   I. Yuval-Davis, Nira II. Anthias, Floya
   III. Campling, Jo
   305.4'2
   ISBN 0–333–45802–8 (hardcover)
   ISBN 0–333–45803–6 (paperback)

Contents

Acknowledgements

This book has its origins in an international workshop organised by Nira Yuval-Davis at Thames Polytechnic in the summer of 1984 on 'Women and National Reproduction', when 20 scholars from about a dozen different countries participated in the three days of discussions which took place at the Dartford short-course centre of the Polytechnic. This provided us with a rare opportunity not only to hear the issues discussed in relation to the different countries, but also to explore together some central questions that both feminist scholarship and theorisations of state and nation have tended to neglect.

We would like to express our gratitude and debt to all the participants in the workshop, – those who eventually contributed to this volume and those who did not. In particular we would like to mention here Judy Kimble who participated in the workshop as part of the Women in South Africa group and whose tragic and untimely death is greatly mourned, and Sylvia Erike who was originally to write the British case study, who has also died since the idea of the book was conceived. We remember and mourn her with appreciation and sadness also.

We should like to express our thanks to Thames Polytechnic, and especially to Dr Greg Koolman, the Head of the School of Social Sciences, and Mr Challinor, the then Assistant Director of the polytechnic, who made this occasion possible.

Special thanks to Jo Campling who gave us much support and encouragement in the preparation of the final manuscript, and to Meirav Dvir who 'slaved' over the word-processor and typed often undecipherable manuscripts.

Finally, we would like to dedicate the book to our children, Gul (Nira), Alexander and Natasha (Floya), without whom we may not have been so aware of some of the complexities involved in the constitution of motherhood, including those which relate to ethnic and national processes.

Notes on the Contributors

Haleh Afshar is a lecturer in politics at the University of York. She was born in Iran and worked with the women's movement there in the 1960s and 1970s. She also worked as a civil servant and a journalist in Teheran until 1974. She has edited *Iran, a Revolution in Turmoil; Women's Work and Ideology in the Third World*; and *Women, State and Ideology* (*also published by Macmillan).

Floya Anthias teaches sociology at Thames Polytechnic, London. She was born in Cyprus but has lived most of her life in Britain. She has researched and written on the political economy of women, on gender, ethnic and class relations, on nationalism and political development in Cyprus, on Cypriot immigrants in Britain and on Cypriot women in the British labour market. She has been involved in the last few years on research into race and the community in south-east London and refugees in Cypriot society. She is currently preparing two books for publication: *Resistance and Control: Racism and the Community* (with H. Cain and N. Yuval-Davis) and *Ethnicity, Class and Migration: Greek-Cypriots in Britain*.

Lesley Caldwell teaches sociology at Thames Polytechnic, London and has been researching and writing on Italy for several years. She is currently preparing a book on women in Italy in the post-war period: *Women between Church and State* which is to be published by Macmillan.

Deborah Gaitskell teaches history at Morley College and for the Workers' Educational Association. She was born in South Africa, educated at the University of Cape Town and has a Ph.D from the School of Oriental and African Studies, London University. She is an editor of the *Journal of Southern African Studies*. She has published on women and Christianity; domestic workers; and girls' education in South Africa. With Elaine Unterhalter, she has run a seminar series entitled 'Women, Colonialism and Commonwealth' at the Institute of Commonwealth Studies, London, for some years.

Deniz Kandiyoti lives and teaches in England. She was a member of the Social Science Departments of the Middle East Technical University in Ankara and Bogazici University in Istanbul between 1969 and

1980. She served as the chairperson of research committee 32 on Women and Society of the International Sociology Association between 1982 and 1986. She is the author of *Women in Rural Production Systems: Problems and Policies* and numerous articles on women and development issues. She is currently working on a volume entitled *Women, Islam and the State*.

Francesca Klug has been active in a number of anti-racism and anti-deportation groups. She was employed as a researcher at the Runnymede Trust from 1980 to 1984 where she worked on a number of publications on racism in Britain. Francesca Klug is co-author of *Worlds Apart: Women under Immigration and Nationality Law* and *New Right, New Racism*.

Marie de Leparvanche is an associate professor in the Department of Anthropology at the University of Sydney. Her fieldwork with Indian immigrants made her confront Australian racism (*Indians in a White Australia*) and her experiences in the patriarchal world of academics opened her eyes to sexism. She remains particularly grateful to the younger women she has worked with who taught her a great deal about the many forms discussion takes. With Gillian Bottomley she edited and contributed to *Ethnicity, Class and Gender in Australia: The Cultural Construction of Race*; and with Barbara Caine and Elizabeth Grosz, *Crossing Boundaries*.

Christine Obbo is an associate professor in anthropology at Wayne State University, Detroit, Michigan and comes from Uganda. Her writings include articles on social change, women and urbanisation, and a book on *African Women*. She has recently compiled a work commissioned by the United Nations on *Migration, Urbanisation and Women in Africa*.

Elaine Unterhalter is a senior research officer in the Department of Sociology at the University of Essex, involved in a project on education in South Africa. Her most recent book is *Forced Removal: The Division, Segregation and Control of the People of South Africa* (1987). She studied at the Universities of the Witwatersrand and Cambridge, then obtained a Ph.D in South African history from the School of Oriental and African Studies, University of London.

Nira Yuval-Davis has been involved in anti-racist and anti-sexist struggles both in Israel and Britain where she teaches sociology at

Thames Polytechnic, London. She is a member of the editorial group of *Khamsin*, a publication forum on the Middle East and has previously co-edited *Israel and the Palestinians* and *Power and the State*. She has researched and written on gender, ethnic and class relations, both in Israel and in Britain; on sexual divisions in the military; on Zionism and Jewish and Palestinian identity; and on Marxism and Jewish nationalism. In the last few years she has also been involved in research on racism and the community in south-east London and is currently preparing for publication (with Floya Anthias and Harriet Cain) *Resistance and Control: Racism and 'the Community'*.

1 Introduction
Floya Anthias and Nira Yuval-Davis

This book offers a range of papers which explore some of the ways women affect and are affected by national and ethnic processes and how these relate to the state. We claim that central dimensions of the roles of women are constituted around the relationships of collectivities to the state. We also claim that central dimensions of the relationships between collectivities and the state are constituted around the roles of women.

Despite the proliferation of literature dedicated to examining and analysing gender divisions in general and women and the state in particular, this central issue finds very little attention. For example, socialist feminists in Britain have insisted that women's position is constructed through various dimensions of state policy. Taxation, social welfare and so on will define women as wives, mothers and workers (Land 1978; Wilson 1977). However, there has been a tendency to treat women as a homogeneous category, or where differences are recognised they are those of class, sexuality, family situation or place in the life-cycle (although not enough work has been done on this either). Issues of ethnicity and nationality have tended to be ignored.

Some change has taken place in this respect, however, with the growth of the Black feminist movement and the critique of the inherent ethnocentrism and racism of Western white feminist theory and practice (Hook 1981). For example, a recent socialist feminist conference which took place in London (spring 1984) included a discussion of immigration legislation, and migrant women, within the sections on women and the state and women and work. Socialist feminists like Michelle Barrett and Mary Mckintosh published their 'Mea Culpa' article in *Feminist Review* (Barrett & Mckintosh 1985) shortly afterwards and the journal itself produced a special issue on Black women (*Feminist Review* 1986). Although this is to be welcomed, other publications (Beechey 1987; Phillips 1987) have 'grafted' the issue of racism onto the analysis of sex and class. This often means that Black and ethnic minority women are marginalised as 'special cases' subjected to social relations, such as those of racist ideology and practice, which are regarded as irrelevant for women in general.

* * *

1

One of the central positions of this book is that national and ethnic processes not only relate to subordinate collectivities but that they constitute a feature of social processes in general, and are therefore relevant to the discussion of majority dominant collectivities.

Before discussing this question with particular reference to women, some general theoretical points need to be made. One important conceptual problem concerns the danger of reifying the 'nation' and the 'ethnic' or 'racial' group, by treating them as totally independent and separate and not considering how they intersect with other modes of differentiation such as class or gender. Much of the dynamic of national strategy for example may be found in the representation of class interests within the nation. However, a great deal of the literature on national and ethnic groups from within a Marxist perspective has taken the connection too far and has tended to reduce ethnic or national groupings to a representation of some form of class grouping. In this way, 'reductionism' is the twin corollary to 'reification' that need to be avoided. A further problem is found in linking the 'interests' of the national and the 'interests' of its male subjects. Any attempt to locate these as identical raises important epistemological and empirical difficulties even where the problematic notion of 'interests' is accepted. Empirically, for example, it is clear that women themselves participate in the oppression and exploitation of women from other ethnic groups as well as from other economic classes. It is important to avoid that form of reductionism which either sees national processes as fundamentally class processes or as representations of generic sexual divisions and conflicts.

The very conceptualisation of 'ethnic' and 'national' groupings and the concepts of ethnic culture, ethnicity and racism have led to much difficulty. Our view is that while we can specify some of the distinguishing features of national and ethnic discourses, they do not have consistent transhistorical contents or effects. Nor can a systematic differentiation be maintained at the general level between them. As a rule, ethnic groups often specify membership as a 'natural' right of being born into them, although there may be other ways of joining. They are usually premised on an assumption concerning a unity of origin among the subjects, whether cultural, historical or biological. A common historical origin or 'fate' and/or shared world of meanings is seen to override the crosscuttings of gender and class. The cultural 'stuff' of ethnic groups always, however, includes a specification of gender and class relations. *National* groups additionally make claims to separate political and territorial representation.

'Ethnicity' and 'nationality' have tended to be either separated or collapsed together in a particular way. In most of the literature available there has often been an assumption, for example, that nationality in terms of 'statehood' and national identity, with its connotations of ethnicity and collective orientation, can be treated as synonymous. On the other hand, 'ethnicity' is often treated in the literature (on the state and on nationalism as well as that on race) as pertaining to minority groups, or subordinate groups within the nation–state.

Theodor Shanin (1986) places this in the context of a 'missing' term in English and French. This missing term in Russian is *natsíonal'nost* (and in Hebrew *Leumiut*). In English and French 'nationality' tends to be synonymous with citizenship, i.e. defines one's legal relationship to a specific state. In Russian and Hebrew, on the other hand, the term does not define a legal relationship but refers to an individual's membership in a collectivity which is inherited from parents. The term 'ethnicity' is the nearest valid equivalent term in English, but Shanin like ourselves (Anthias & Yuval-Davis 1983) emphasises that it is not a characteristic limited only to minority or subordinate groups, but constitutes a major parameter of social relationships. As such its relationship to the state has to be problematised and theorised, and not assumed.

THE BOUNDARIES OF THE STATE

One major issue in this context is the delineation of the boundary between 'the state' and 'the nation'. There is the further problem of delineating the state from the economy and the gamut of social institutions, social groups and relations that may be conceptualised as part of 'civil society' (Urry 1981). The tendency in much of the literature on the state to identify it with 'the nation' is linked to the historical fact that nationalism in the West has been a central force in the development of the nation–state. The ensuing conflation of the boundary of the state with that of the nation fails to recognise that state processes can be more delimited than national processes. There are often groups of subjects (minorities; and sometimes as in South Africa, majorities) that are excluded from participation in the state or are a special focus of state concerns as well national liberation struggles by minorities who reside in more than one state (like the Kurds or the Palestinians). Nor does it take account of the opposite, that is that the state can extend beyond the boundary of the nation, so that the nation–state form may be replaced by a supranational structure as, for example, potentially lies in the European Community.

Concerning the concept of the state, we find similar problems to those mentioned earlier, of reification on the one hand, treating the state as totally autonomous, and reductionism on the other (seeing the state as representing the interests essentially of specific economic classes, such as within certain versions of Marxism (Jessop 1982)). This issue relates both to the boundary between the state and the economy and to that of civil society in as much as it leads us to ask who and what social forces construct the political project(s) of the state and in what way or sense is it a neutral vehicle in itself which can be used as an instrument by various social forces.

Before we consider the links between the state and civil society and how they relate to whom it is pertinent to briefly note a number of influential developments in the conceptualisation of the state and civil society.

Most of these developments have tended to broaden out the conception of the state away from seeing it purely as a managerial structure, on the one hand, or as centrally dedicated to repression, coercion, force and social control, on the other. There has been a shift towards looking at the state as incorporating a number of institutions whose role appears strictly private and/or primarily 'ideological' (such as the church, the family, the school, the media etc.) – a tradition whose origins are in Gramsci but also in the Althusserian and Poulantzian tradition of social analysis (Mouffe 1979; Laclau 1979). Secondly there has been a tendency to see the state as the place where the global interests of capital are expressed, either in the sense of capital accumulation (as in the capital logic school – see CSE London Edinburgh Group 1979) or in the sense of the state as co-ordinating the different interests and activities of fractions of capital (as in Poulantzas 1973, 1976). The main difficulty here lies in being able to specify the mechanisms or intentionality at work and the processes by which they are achieved, a particular problem faced by any form of functionalism. This approach is similar in form if not in content to seeing the state as an arena within which different social forces can articulate their interests and therefore as a kind of battleground where, however, for the functionalist the winner is always already known! Finally, partly as a result of some of the theoretical and empirical difficulties involved in specifying the state, a further tendency has been to reject the idea of a unitary state and focus on social policies, the law, institutional arrangements and discourses as heterogeneous elements which are not reducible to 'the state' (Sassoon 1987). This work has rightly pointed out that the effects of these practices neither emanate from a given primary source nor do they have unitary effects.

Having sketched out very briefly the terms of reference in some of the writings on the state, we can now return first to the issue of the links between the state and civil society and second to the relationship specifically with gender divisions and women. We share the view that the state is neither unitary in its practices, its intentions nor its effects. Nonetheless, we feel it is useful to retain the concept of the state. The term refers to a particular 'machinery' for the exercise of 'government' over a given population, usually territorially and nationally defined, although the definitions of what constitutes these boundaries etc. will shift and change depending on what it is government or power over and what is being managed or negotiated. Hence we can specify the state in terms of a body on institutions which are centrally organised around the intentionality of control with a given apparatus of enforcement at its command and basis. Coercion and repression are then to be seen both as forms of control and as a back-up. Different forms of the state will involve different relationships between the control/coercion twin which is the residing characteristic of the state. Using this formulation, the state can harness a number of different processes, including ideological ones, through juridical and repressive mechanisms at its command. Education and the media are the prime institutional forms for ideological production in the modern liberal–democratic state but they are not part of the state as such.

Civil society includes those institutions, collectivities, groupings and social agonies which lie outside the formal rubric of state parameters as outlined but which both informs and is informed by them. This includes the family, social strata, ethnic and national groupings to note some of the most significant, as well as institutions like those of education, trade unions and the means of communication like the media. These produce their own ideological contents as well as being subjected to those of the state. In this way ideology does not reside (in a privileged sense) in either civil society or the state nor is it monolithic in terms of its contents. There is a question regarding, however, the degree to which the state is able to tolerate those forms that conflict with its political project. Again, different forms of the state and different historical and regional differences exist worldwide in this respect.

Indeed to avoid both a static essentialism and functionalism, it is important to consider the state both in terms of its intentions and in terms of its effects. This involves looking at the specific political projects of states and the economic and social context within which they are articulated as well as the social forces that both construct and oppose them.

WOMEN, THE STATE AND NATIONAL/ETHNIC PROCESSES

Women's link to the state is complex. On the one hand, they are acted upon as members of collectivities, institutions or groupings, and as participants in the social forces that give the state its given political projects in any particular social and historical context. On the other hand, they are a special focus of state concerns as a social category with a specific role (particularly human reproduction). It is important to note, however, that these roles cannot be understood in relation to the state reproducing itself, or that any absolute control by the state would be achievable, given women's incorporation at a number of other social levels within civil society and in the economy.

A number of attempts (Pateman 1986; Saraceno 1987) to conceptualise the link between women and the state have focused on the central dimension of citizenship and how, far from being gender-neutral, it constructs men and women differently. Thus the feminist and socialist feminist critique of the state and state theorisation has advanced from one which points to the way the state *treats* women unequally in relation to men. There now exists a theoretical critique of the way the very project of the welfare state itself has constituted the 'state subject' in a gendered way, that is as essentially male in its capacities and needs. However, different forms of the state and different states even within the same form, involve the positing of a different constituency for 'citizenship'. The notion of citizenship focuses on the way the *state* acts upon the *individual* and does not address the problem of the way in which the state itself forms its political project. Therefore it cannot on its own attend to the social forces and movements that are hegemonic within the state. This applies also to the state's relationship to women. 'Citizenship', on its own, does not encapsulate adequately the relations of control and negotiation that take place in a number of different arenas of social life.

When we come to discuss the ways women affect and are affected by national and ethnic processes within civil society, and the ways these relate to the state, it is important to remember that there is no unitary category of women which can be unproblematically conceived as the focus of ethnic, national or state policies and discourses. Women are divided along class, ethnic and life-cycle lines and in most societies different strategies are directed at different groups of women. This is the case both from within the ethnic collectively and from the state, whose boundaries virtually always contain a number of ethnicities.

While we have argued against the links between women, the state and ethnic/national processes taking any necessary form we can nevertheless locate five major (although not exclusive) ways in which women have tended to participate in ethnic and national processes and in relation to state practices. These are:

(a) as biological reproducers of members of ethnic collectivities;
(b) as reproducers of the boundaries of ethnic/national groups;
(c) as participating centrally in the ideological reproduction of the collectivity and as transmitters of its culture;
(d) as signifiers of ethnic/national differences – as a focus and symbol in ideological discourses used in the construction, reproduction and transformation of ethnic/national categories;
(e) as participants in national, economic, political and military struggles.

Different historical contexts will construct these roles not only in different ways but also the centrality of these roles will differ.

Before giving a further explication of the above categories, a word of caution is necessary in relation to the use of the term 'reproduction'. We consider this concept as problematic on more than one ground. First of all, its use in the literature includes many and indeed inconsistent meanings, from a definition of women's biological role to explanations of the existence of social systems over time (e.g. Edholm *et al*. 1976; Hindess & Hirst 1975).

Even more importantly, the term 'reproduction' has been criticised as being tautological on the one hand, often implicitly assuming that 'reproduction' takes place, and static on the other hand, therefore unable to explain growth, decline and transformation processes (women act as both maintainers and modifiers of social processes).

By retaining the term 'reproduction', however, in the depiction of some of the then central roles women play we wished to locate our work in relation to the literature which deals with human and social reproduction. Feminist literature on 'reproduction' has dealt with biological reproduction, the reproduction of labour power or state citizenship, but has generally failed to consider the reproduction of national, ethnical and racial categories. (See, for example, Edholm *et al.* 1976; O'Brien 1981; a notable exception has been WING 1985; see also Yuval-Davis 1980, 1982, Anthias 1983.)

We shall now describe in more detail the range of policies and discourses which can be included in each of the five categories noted earlier.

(a) As biological reproducers of members of ethnic collectivities

Various forms of population control are the most obvious policies which relate to women as biological reproducers of members of collectivities. The fear of being 'swamped' by different racial or ethnic groups has given rise to both individual state and interstate policies which are aimed at limiting the physical numbers of members of groups that are defined as 'undesirable'. One form these take is represented most clearly in immigration controls. More extreme measures are the physical expulsion of particular groups and even actual extermination of them (e.g. Jews and gypsies in Nazi Germany). A further strategy is to limit the number of people born within specific ethnic groups by controlling the reproductive capacity and activity of women. These range from forced sterilisation to the massive mobilisation of birth control campaigns. The other facet of such a concern is the active encouragement of population growth of the 'right kind', i.e. of the ethnic group dominant in the state apparatus. Calls for a 'White Australia' immigration policy or Jewish 'return' to Israel are supplemented at times of slack immigration or national crisis with active calls for women to bear more children so that no 'demographic holocaust' will take place. This encouragement is very often a question of using national and religious discourses about the duty of women to produce more children. (A popular Palestinian saying in Israel for example boasts that 'The Israelis beat us at the borders but we beat them in the bedrooms'.) However, in many cases, rather than relying on ideological mobilisation, the state establishes child benefit systems and other maternal benefits such as loans to this purpose. (The Beveridge Report for example cited fear for the fate of the 'British race' as the major reason for establishing child benefits in Britain.)

(b) As reproducers of the boundaries of ethnic/national groups

Women are controlled not only by being encouraged or discouraged from having children who will become members of the various ethnic groups within the state. They are also controlled in terms of the 'proper' way in which they should have them – i.e. in ways which will reproduce the boundaries of the symbolic identity of their group or that of their husbands. In some cases (as until recently in South Africa) women are not allowed to have sexual relations with men of other groups. This particularly is the case for dominant-group women. Legal marriage is generally a condition if the child is to be recognised as a member of the group and very often religious and social traditions dictate who can marry whom so that the character as well as the boundaries of the group can be maintained from one generation to the other. In Israel, for example, it is the mother who determines whether or not the child will be considered Jewish. But if the mother is already married (or even divorced, but only by civil rather than by religious law) to another man, that child will be an outcast and not allowed to marry another Jew. In Egypt, on the other hand, a child born to a Muslim woman and a Copt Christian man will have no legal status.

(c) As participating centrally in the ideological reproduction of the collectivity and as the transmitters of its culture

The role of women as ideological reproducers is very often related to women being seen as the 'cultural carriers' of the ethnic group. Women are the main socialisers of small children but in the case of ethnic minorities they are often less assimilated socially and linguistically within the wider society. They may be required to transmit the rich heritage of ethnic symbols and ways of life to the other members of the ethnic group, especially the young.

(d) As signifiers of ethnic/national differences

Women do not only teach and transfer the cultural and ideological traditions of ethnic and national groups. Very often they constitute their actual symbolic figuration. The nation as a loved woman in danger or as a mother who lost her sons in battle is a frequent part of the particular nationalist discourse in national liberation struggles or other forms of national conflicts when men are called to fight 'for the sake of our women and children' or to 'defend their honour'. Often the distinction between one ethnic group and another is constituted centrally by the sexual behaviour of women. For example a 'true' Sikh or Cypriot girl should behave in sexually appropriate ways. If she does not then neither her children nor herself may be considered part of the community (Anthias & Yuval-Davis 1983).

(e) As participants in national, economic, political and military struggles

Finally, and probably the category that requires least explication is the role that women have come to play in national and ethnic struggles. Women's role in national liberation struggles, in guerilla warfare or in the military has varied, but generally they are seen to be in a supportive and nurturing relation to men even where they have taken most risks (Yuval-Davis 1985). In addition, the way in which national liberation struggles have articulated issues concerning gender divisions and women's liberation is a consideration here.

The explication of some of the central roles that women play in relation to national and ethnic processes must bear in mind three important elements. The first relates to the link between national/ethnic processes and the state. We have noted already that the relationship between collectivities and the state is complex and will vary in different historical and social contexts. Whilst only rarely exclusively so, customary and religious norms and legislation, which usually construct women as primarily biological reproducers, will often be incorporated and reinforced by state legislation, although contradictions can exist also between state and religious legislation. Thus the sphere of 'civil society' and the sphere of the 'state' can link hands in the construction of women in some ways although in others they might be in conflict. In addition, the political projects of the state are often the outcome of tensions and conflicts within civil society and are carried by social classes or other social forces (Molyneux 1985; Kandiyoti 1987). In addition, the state will often identify and specify those groupings or social relations that it can legislate on but which it delineates as private and therefore essentially as an individual matter of choice or liberty in its specifics. Such is the case in relation to the family, for example. When we look at the role of women as markers of collective boundaries and differences and also as participants in national, political and economic struggles we often find a contradiction – women are constituted through the state but are also often actively engaged in countering state processes.

Secondly, the central role that women play should not lead us to the fallacy that women are attended to either only as women (i.e. in their 'difference' from men) or that all women, irrespective of class, age or family situation are attended to in the same way. Often there may indeed be tension between, on the one hand, treating women as 'different', say in certain of their capacities or potentialities, and treating them 'equally' in others (e.g. as workers). Also an 'equal' treatment by the state in any number of capacities will not necessarily lead to the destruction of a sexual division of labour in society more generally. Notions of what are specifically women's needs or duties often reassert themselves in very traditional ways even in revolutionary societies. This clearly requires the much wider discussion of gender relations. There is no space here to review some of the central positions taken in this regard but we argue elsewhere (Anthias & Yuval-Davis 1983) that gender divisions are irreducible to class or other divisions. Clearly, for the purpose of our argument here it is important to note that the state does not exclusively construct gender divisions nor can they be seen only in the context of any specific state mechanisms at any historical moment as they relate to the whole are of gender 'differentiation'.

In addition, we find it vitally important to emphasise that the roles that women play are not merely imposed upon them. Women actively participate in the process of reproducing and modifying their roles as well as being actively involved in controlling other women.

Finally, we would like to end with an Australian poem which points poignantly at one of women's central roles in times of national crisis:

> Ye girls of British race
> Famous for your beauty
> Breed fast in all your grace
> For this is your duty.
> As Anzac gave in war
> So daughters at your call

Will quick respond the more
To replace those that fall.[1]

*   *   *

The various contributions to this book examine the relationship
between women, the national and the state in the specificity of their
particular societies at a given historical moment. As such they
concentrate on, or emphasise, only one or two of the dimensions we
have explored in this introduction – those that they find most central
in the historical contexts of the states and societies they describe.

Francesca Klug in the British case study concentrates on the way
women's roles have been affected by the changing nature and
boundaries of the British national collectivity. The 'myth of the one
British nation' has postulated that women are its members essentially
in and through their relations with men, as dependants, particularly
in their capacity as wives and mothers. The autonomous right of
women to belong to the 'nation' has been particularly denied under
immigration and nationality law and in welfare state policy. She
illustrates clearly the ways in which racism and sexism have intersec-
ted in the construction of the myth of British collective identity and
shows that 'Britain for the white British' has been the result, to a
great extent, of deliberate state policy.

By examining the history of immigration and population policies in
Australia, Marie de Lepervanche's chapter looks at the ways in which
the notion of Australian citizenship is gender-specific and how
women are constructed differently from men by Australian state
policies, mainly as breeders of the nation and as keepers of communal boundaries. However, Marie de Lepervanche goes on to show
that womanhood as such is not a unitary category, and women of
different ethnic racial and class positions are constructed differently
in Australia.

Deborah Gaitskell and Elaine Unterhalter's article on South
Africa compares the notion of motherhood as it has been constructed
and used by Afrikaner nationalism and in the African National
Congress. In both cases ideologies of women as mothers have played
a central role within the national mobilisation processes. However, as
this chapter points out, the notion of motherhood is a very fluid and
manipulable one. Its historical construction in these two cases is
greatly affected by the very different state and class contexts as well

as the different constructions of race and nation found within the two movements.

Christine Obbo's contribution on Uganda illustrates the manner in which discourses around women's sexuality, particularly in respect to notions about 'the proper woman' and 'reproductive potential' are central to notions of what it is to be a good and loyal member of the Ugandan collectivity. She shows, however, how discourses around women's primary role as 'mother' are often used as weapons to prevent women's equal participation with men as workers and citizens.

Nira Yuval-Davis considers the ways in which women have been constructed as national reproducers in Israel both ideologically, as markers of the category of 'who is a Jew', and biologically, as suppliers of human power of the 'right kind'. She focuses particularly on debates around demographic policies in Israel and the ways in which they relate to specific ways with which the establishment of the Israeli state through the zionist movement has constructed the Israeli Jewish collectivity.

Haleh Afshar shows firstly how, with the use of fundamentalism in Iran, women have been directed towards domesticity, and secondly how the family and motherhood have been defined as the kernel of 'nationhood'. Through an examination of the political, religious and economic forces at work in the contemporary period, the links between the control of women and the rise of Iranian nationalism are explained.

Deniz Kandiyoti's writing on Turkey provides an analytical and historical account of the reforms constituted in the formation of the secular Turkish state after 1923. She concentrates on the way in which the issue of women's emancipation was used in the construction of the new nation. The main pivot of her argument is that 'the woman question' in Turkey was part of the ideological means by which Turkish national identity was articulated and debated.

In her article on the Greek-Cypriot experience in Cyprus, Floya Anthias considers the ways in which women have been linked to ethnic and nationalist discourse and practice in a small and now ethnically and territorially divided society. She pays attention to the way in which notions of women's sexuality and mothering roles are related to ethnic exclusivity and the maintenance of the ethnic boundary. She analyses the ways in which the contemporary Greek-Cypriot state of Cyprus uses discourses and practices around women to pursue 'the ethnic question' and to articulate its political project.

Finally, Lesley Caldwell's article on Italy looks at the way in which the category of women has been established as a separate constituency fundamental to the construction of a new Italian nation in its post-fascist form. By looking at statements made in the Constituent Assembly, the Italian Communist Party and the Union of Italian Women, Lesley Caldwell is able to show how 'the woman issue' has been used to give a progressive stamp to the new republic, while at the same time more traditional notions of women in the family, especially as mothers, have been central in the process of national mobilisation.

NOTE

1.   Quoted by M. de Lepervanche in this volume from McQueen, *Social Sketches of Australia 1888–1975* (Harmondsworth: Penguin, 1978), p.158.

BIBLIOGRAPHY

Anthias, F. (1983) 'Sexual Divisions and Ethnic Adaptation', in A. Phizacklea (ed.), *One Way Ticket* (London: Routledge & Kegan Paul).
Anthias, F. & N. Yuval-Davis (1983) 'Contextualising Feminism – Gender, Ethnic and Class Divisions', *Feminist Review*, no. 15, 62–76.
Barrett, M. (1987) 'The Concept of Difference', *Feminist Review* no. 26, 24–42.
Barrett, M. & M. Mckintosh (1985) 'Ethnocentrism and Socialist–Feminist Theory', *Feminist Review* no. 20, 23–48.
Beechey, V. (1987) *Unequal Work* (London: Verso).
CSE London Edinburgh Group (1979) *In and Against the State* (London: Pluto).
Edholm, F., O. Harris & K. Young (1976) 'Conceptualizing Women', *Critique of Anthropology*, vol. 3, no. 9, 101–30.
Hindess, B. & P. Hirst (1975) *Pre-Capitalist Modes of Production* (London: Routledge & Kegan Paul).
Hooks, B. (1981) *Ain't I a Woman – Black Women and Feminism* (Boston: Southend Press).
Jessop, B. (1982) *The Capitalist State (London: Martin Robertson)*.
Kandiyoti, D. (1987) 'Emancipated but Unliberated? Reflections on the Turkish Case', Feminist Studies, vol. 13, no. 2, 317–88.

Laclau, E. (ed.) (1979) *Politics and Ideology in Marxist Theory* (London: New Left Books).

Land, H. (1978) 'Sex Role Stereotyping in the Social Security and Income Tax Systems', in J. Chetwynd and O. Hartnett (eds), *The Sex Role System* (London: Routledge & Kegan Paul).

Molyneux, M. (1985) 'Women in Socialist Societies: Theory and Practice', in K. Young, C. Wolkowitz and R. McCullagh (eds), *Of Marriage and the Market* (London: CSE Books) 167–202.

Mouffe, C. (cd.) (1979) *Gramsci and Marxist Theory* (London: Routledge & Kegan Paul).

O'Brien, M. (1981) *The Politics of Reproduction* (London: Routledge & Kegan Paul).

Pateman, C. (1986) 'Feminism and Participatory Democracy', paper given to *American Philosophical Association*, Missouri, May 1986.

Phillips, A. (1987) *Divided Loyalties* (London: Pluto).

Poulantzas, N. (1973) *Political Power and Social Classes* (London: New Left Books).

Poulantzas, N. (1976) 'The Capitalist State – a Reply to Miliband and Laclau', *New Left Review*, no. 95, 68–83.

Saraceno, C. (1987) 'Gender in the Construction of Citizenship', paper given to workshop on women and the state, Berlin 29th June–1 July.

Sassoon, A. (ed.) (1987) *Women and the State* (London: Hutchinson).

Shanin, T. (1986) 'Soviet Concepts of Ethnicity: The Case of a Missing Term', *New Left Review*, No. 158, 113–22.

Urry, J. (1981) *The Anatomy of Capitalist Societies* (London: Macmillan).

Wilson, E. (1977) *Women and the Welfare State* (London: Tavistock).

WING (1985) *Worlds Apart, Women under Immigration and Nationality Law* (London: Pluto).

Yuval-Davis, N. (1980) 'The Bearers of the Collective: Women and Religious Legislation in Israel', *Feminist Review*, no. 4, 15–27.

Yuval-Davis, N. (1982) 'National Reproduction: Sexism, Racism and the State', paper given to British Sociological Association, annual conference, April.

Yuval-Davis, N. (1985) 'Front and Rear: the Sexual Division of Labour in the Israeli Army', *Feminist Studies*, vol. 2, no. 3, 649–76.

2   'Oh to be in England': the British Case Study

Francesca Klug

INTRODUCTION

The British nation state is a myth. It has never really existed. Not, that is, in the literal sense of one national group bound together through a common ancestry and/or heritage, living in one political entity called a state. Indeed, there is no modern state which is not multi-racial or multi-national in character. In Britain there has been an attempt to construct the nation around the myth of a continuous line of Anglo-Saxon people with unique rights to claim Britain as their 'homeland'. In reality the British Isles have for centuries been inhabited by a variety of peoples with different cultural, linguistic, racial and even national identities. At the same time, because of Britain's imperial history, those who did come to share a common British identity and/or citizenship (characteristics generally associated with nationhood) have not all lived in the UK but have been scattered around the world – their access to the rights which flow from citizenship dependent on their ancestry or race.

Within this historical development women have been cast in a particular role. Categorised as 'dependants', as essentially wives and mothers, they have been denied access to some of the rights afforded to men under immigration and nationality law. While at certain periods white British women have been actively encouraged to reproduce for the nation, at others a series of measures have explicitly sought to curb the size of the black British population.

This chapter explores the way that the intersection of racism and gender differentiation have found expression in the construction of the British nation. Constraints of space and time have prevented me from examining the responses of women, black people or immigrants to the developments described. Similar constraints have prevented more than a passing reference to the development of the British nation in relation to the people of Scotland, Wales and Ireland. The emphasis is almost entirely on how the British state has treated 'aliens' and black British subjects (for an analysis of the former, see Nairn 1977).

EXPANSION AND IMPERIALISM

Pre-feudal England was colonised by Celts, Romans, Germans (Anglo-Saxons), Danes (Vikings) and finally Normans. Attempts to ward off each round of conquerors were doomed. But eventually something approximating a common English identity was forged through a combination of shared experience, the fusion of different tongues into the English language and the practical constraints of living side by side.

As Norman feudalism took root, England itself became a colonising power, expanding its hold over the peoples of Scotland, Wales and Ireland. England became Great Britain in 1707, following the Act of Union with Scotland, and in 1801 the 'United Kingdom of Great Britain and Ireland' was created – a title reflecting a statement of intent as much as a constitutional change. In reality disunity has repeatedly threatened this arrangement. From the seventeenth century onwards British military expansion extended far beyond these shores. By the time that the 'nation–state' form was developing in Europe, following the collapse of the old empires, British territories covered a quarter of the earth's land surface.

It was not until the decades following the Second World War that Britain took on a form that even approximated that of modern nation or unitary state. By this time most of the former colonies had fought for and gained their independence, and UK citizens – black and white – were settled all over the world.

IMMIGRATION, NATIONALITY AND RACISM

The 1914 British Nationality and Status of Aliens Act the first of the modern British nationality Acts created a common status of British subject[1] for all inhabitants of the Empire. But its aim was *not* to signify that all British subjects, both rulers and ruled, were equal before God and the Crown. Quite the contrary, it was introduced to put the seal on British domination, to emphasise the incorporation of the colonised into the British state. A form of apartheid operated in the settler colonies like India and Rhodesia, with enormous distinctions between the rights of black and white British subjects.

But under Britain's nationality laws there was no legal distinction between people born in the UK and any other part of the Empire.

Who was and who was not considered to be part of the British nation was quite a separate matter from the legal category of British subject. The equality contained in the 1914 Act in no way detracted from the absolute faith the British ruling class had in their superiority over those they ruled, which derived from the supposed Anglo-Saxon origins of the 'British'. This brand of British nationalism grew in tandem with the Empire and by the end of the nineteenth century it had filtered down to be widely accepted in popular consciousness. When Colonial Secretary, Sir Edward Lytton, told MPs in 1858 that their destiny was 'to fulfil the mission of the Anglo-Saxon race in spreading intelligence, freedom and Christian faith' (Hansard, vol.151, col.1821) he was speaking in the idiom of the times.

Racism, and especially the pseudo-scientific type of racism which saw blacks as genetically inferior to whites was central to the nationalism which flourished along with the British Empire. This acted as the ideological defence of British imperialism. It was racism which provided the lynch pin for Britain's immigration and nationality laws which sought to control entry to the British Isles and define membership of the British nation.

The nineteenth century witnessed a considerable increase in immigration to Britain. Under English rule famine and poverty drove over half of the Irish population to emigrate in the century after 1820. Most of them went to the United States and England. Jewish immigrants from eastern Europe followed hard on their heels. Between 1870 and 1914 about 120,000 Jews came to Britain to escape persecution and massacres in tsarist Russia and the surrounding countries.

The Jewish refugees met hostility and discrimination when they arrived. A sustained campaign for immigration control developed which was without precedent in British history. An unholy alliance of Tory MPs, promised socialists, trade union leaders and members of the crypto-fascist British Brothers' League lobbied for the 'flood' of immigrants to be stopped. Eventually, the 1905 Aliens Act was passed subjecting all non-British subjects to immigration control for the first time.

Notwithstanding the specifically anti-semitic nature of the call for immigration control, the explanation as to why this clamour developed at this particular period is surely tied up with the nationalism induced by the experience of empire. In this context 'outsiders' like 'alien Jews' had to be excluded from the British nation, while 'primitive blacks' had to be ruled by it. Indeed 'aliens' and 'blacks' provided the foil against which the British nation was defined.

A slightly different picture started to emerge with the decline of the British Empire. After the Second World War in particular, more and more territories fought for and won their independence, although most continued to be part of the Commonwealth and as such their citizens were still subjects of the Crown.

The all-inclusive legal definition of British nationality as created by the 1914 British Nationality Act (and reinforced by the twilight-of-Empire 1948 Act)[2] became less and less compatible with this new reality. For a while this contradiction was not particularly problematic for the British state. Postwar Britain, like most other industrialised countries, urgently needed cheap migrant labour for its expanding economy. Immigrants from the colonies and Commonwealth countries provided a major and convenient source for this labour power.

However, when it became clear that not only was Britain's economy starting to contract, but also that black Commonwealth immigrants were increasingly claiming their rights as British subjects to settle permanently in Britain, the shared legal status of black and white British subjects was rapidly removed. This was achieved through immigration legislation, whilst the increasingly tenuous myth of a common citizenship for black and white Britons was maintained by, for the time being, leaving British nationality legislation intact.

Successive governments in the 1960s passed a series of immigration Acts which progressively reduced the status of black British subjects to one which approximated that of 'aliens'. Under the explicitly racist principle of patriality, introduced by the 1971 Immigration Act, broadly speaking only those British subjects who were born in the British Isles and their descendants (that is basically white people) were entitled to settle in Britain.[3] The gap between British immigration and nationality legislation was finally closed by the 1981 Nationality Act which essentially linked the patriality principle to British nationality. Those British subjects not eligible, on grounds of birth or descent, for full British citizenship literally became second-class citizens. As British Dependent Territories Citizens or British Overseas Citizens they have no right whatsoever to live in Britain.[4]

Running in parallel with these developments has been the rise of a different kind of anti-black racism – that has come to be known as the 'new racism' (Barker 1981). This relies not so much on the view that black people are inferior but instead on the premise that different cultural groups simply do not mix. If the old variant, with its emphasis on the intellectual superiority of white people, acted as a suitable legitimation of imperial rule, the new brand provides the ideological justification for separation in the form of strict immigration controls (although there are still many fanatically racist and nationalist groups which peddle with crude notions of 'inferior stock').

In recent years this new brand of racism has appeared regularly – almost casually and in passing – as if it is just common sense. The *Daily Star*'s commentator Robert McNeill argued on 17 April 1984 that 'any fool knows . . . that the process which Darwin called natural selection means that, on the whole, people prefer their "ain folk" – their own ethnic stock', while feature writer Jill Tweedie wrote in the *Guardian* that 'so much is a kind of racism built into humanity that it could well be considered a primeval, possibly genetic, inheritance from our most distant ancestors, of whatever race or colour' (24 January 1984). Of course it was this kind of theme which Prime Minister Margaret Thatcher was developing when she said in a television interview in 1978 that 'People are really rather afraid that this country might be rather swamped by people with a different culture and . . . if there is any fear that it might be swamped people are going to react and be rather hostile to those coming in.'

In practical terms the 'new racism' has both fuelled and legitimised the most stringent immigration controls to date. At the last two general elections the government boasted that immigration was lower than at any time since controls for Commonwealth citizens were introduced in 1962; Tamil and Iranian refugees are regularly refused asylum; and, most recently, there is the new Immigration Bill which will remove the automatic right of women and children to join their husbands and fathers who immigrated to Britain before the 1971 Immigration Act was passed.

But for some advocates of the 'new racism' this is still not enough. However tight, immigration controls cannot stop black people already living here from having children. The only 'solution', from this point of view, is to make black people 'go home'. It is not only fascists who promote this view. Enoch Powell MP has done so for decades. Others on the far right of the Conservative Party, such as members of the Monday Club's Immigration and Race Relations Committee, have increasingly pushed for a policy of so-called 'voluntary repatriation' particularly in the context of inner city strife (Gordon & Klug 1986).

EUGENICS AND THE PATRIARCHAL NATION

Racist ideologies and in particular those based on pseudo-scientific notions of innate superiority, have been linked to the construction of gender relations. This link was particularly strong in Britain's imperial days and focused around the eugenicist notions of selective breeding and genetic inheritance. These were based on the supposed need, as leading eugenicist Prof. Karl Pearson put it, to create a 'reserve of brain and physique' (Fryer 1984: 181). Such ideas became increasingly influential around the turn of the century as the relatively poor British military performance in the Boer Wars brought fears of 'national inefficiency' and 'unhealthy stock'. Through this, public attention became focused on the destitute state in which the working class lived. Concern grew over the supposedly 'lowering effect' on 'British stock' of uncontrolled breeding by the working class. As middle and upper class families were more likely to have access to information on birth control, the eugenicists were concerned that they would be 'swamped' by the working class. The consequence, as they saw it, would be that Britain would eventually be unable to compete with other industrial powers and, worse still, would lose its eminence among nations.

To safeguard the health of the nation eugenicists gave women, or rather middle class women, a pivotal role. The elevation of motherhood was emphasised at the expense of women developing other skills. In a lecture on 'The Woman's Question' in 1885, for example, Pearson stated that 'Those nations which have been the most reproductive have, on the whole, been the ruling nations . . . if child-bearing women must be intellectually handicapped then the penalty to be paid for race-predominance is the subjection of women' (Semmel 1960: ch.2).

Given the central role allocated to women as physical reproducers of the nation by the prevailing ideology of the time, it is not surprising that nineteenth- and twentieth-century British nationality law was explicitly patriarchal. Firstly, women were only allowed to reproduce the British nation on behalf of their husbands. They could not pass on their nationality to their children in their own right. So if an unmarried British woman gave birth to a child outside the British Empire he or she would be born stateless. (But, for reasons already explained, any child born within the British Empire regardless of parentage, would automatically be a British subject.) Secondly, a woman's own nationality was determined by that of her husband. If she married an 'alien', that is a man without British subject status, she was defined 'out' of the British nation and was expected to take on the nationality of her spouse (in practice she could only do so if she married a man whose country's citizenship laws provided this facility). At the same time, a 'foreign' woman who married a British man automatically entered the fold – she did not have to go through a naturalisation process to become British.

The patriarchal nature of British nationality law was actually strengthened in the late nineteenth century. It was the 1870 Naturalisation Act which was the first to explicitly state that a British woman was deemed an 'alien' if her husband was not British (although generally speaking under Common Law such women tended to be treated as 'foreigners' anyway). Although suffragettes and feminists campaigned for this to be amended by the 1914 Nationality Act, the all-male parliament stood firm. In the words of Lewis Hardcourt, Secretary of State for the Colonies, to allow a woman to retain her own nationality 'when she deliberately marries an alien' would be 'departing from the practice of the whole civilized world . . . with the exception of Venezuela and Spain' (WING 1985: 14).

It was not until 1948 that women won the right to retain their nationality on marriage – three decades after women over 30 got the vote. And it was not until 1981 that they won the right to transfer their citizenship to their own children born abroad. In addition to eugenistic notions on the role of women, ideological factors similar to those which led to immigration control being introduced in Britain for the first time at the turn of the century helped to shape the patriarchal nature of British nationality law. As already noted, the common status conferred on all subjects of the Empire by the 1914 Act was to mark their incorporation into British rule. If there had to be coherence in the Empire all the more so in the family! Opponents of equality in nationality law argued that as men were the head of the family they must define its national identity. If a woman married 'out' then she automatically put herself outside the nation. Otherwise, so the argument ran, there could be anarchy with women claiming dual citizenship. If this were the case no clear demarcation would exist between those who did and those who did not owe loyalty to the British state and the Empire.

SOCIAL POLICY AND THE RISE AND FALL OF THE BRITISH BIRTH RATE

The question of the reproduction of the nation also had a profound effect on the development of social policy with regard to women and reproduction in this period. There was a school of eugenics, many fabian–socialists included, which argued that for the sake of the British nation the population *as a whole* needed boosting both in terms of quality and of quantity – and that programmes to encourage population growth should not be restricted to the middle and upper classes. Once again the role of women was crucial in this scheme. In the fabian tract of 1907, for example, fabian leader Sidney Webb argued for the 'endowment of motherhood' – that is, financial recognition by the state that child-bearing was for the national good.

This era saw the dawning of what came to be known as the welfare state. The 1906 Liberal government introduced a series of new social reforms (Fraser 1975). In addition to a genuinely held Liberal commitment to boosting the living standards of the poor, the state was concerned to improve the physical well-being of the population as a whole to make the British people fit defenders of the Empire. At the same time 'aliens' were to be denied access to these new benefits. Under major pieces of legislation introduced around the turn of the century eligibility for welfare depended upon immigration status (Cohen 1985). Among the new reforms were policies aimed at encouraging women to breed and at improving the health of their offspring, such as the introduction of maternity insurance, health visitors and child welfare.

At the same time what amounted to a national panic set in over the declining British birth rate, particularly after the First World War. It began to fall from the late 1870s onwards and by 1933 it was at its lowest point yet. Demographic experts were predicting that the time was approaching when the British population would be down to 16 million. The extent of the anxiety around this related to Britain's continued imperial role. In 1935 Prime Minister Neville Chamberlain warned that the time would come when 'the British Empire will be crying out for more citizens of the right breed and when we in this country shall not be able to supply the demand' (Rowbotham 1973: p. 144).

Books like *The Twilight of Parenthood* and *The Menace of British Depopulation* predicted national decline. In 1944, in an essay entitled 'The English People', George Orwell lamented the fact that 'Britain today has a million and a half fewer children than in 1914' and advocated a more graduated system of taxation 'to encourage child bearing and to save young children from being obliged to work outside the home' (Riley 1981: 89). Such views were typical of those to be found in a range of periodicals, books and speeches of the time.

In 1943 the issue of how to reverse the decline in the national birth rate was discussed in both Houses of Parliament. Methods proposed ranged from elevating the status of motherhood in a generalised way to providing financial and social inducement to make child-rearing less onerous. Finally in 1944 a Royal Commission on Population was set up.

It took five years for the Commission to report. By this time there had in fact been a reverse in the trend and the birth rate increased substantially from 1941 onwards. This was noted by the Commission but it nevertheless warned that if this was not maintained the population would seriously decline. This in turn threatened Britain's imperial rule, its wealth and the future development of the world.

> The growth of population in Great Britain was in fact an essential condition not only of the development of Britain itself, but also of the growth of the new overseas countries inhabited mainly or largely by people of British descent, and of the spread of British culture and influence all over the world through emigrants, commerce and capital investment. (Royal Commission on Population 1949: ch.2)

The solution advocated by the Commission to avoid the impending doom of a declining British population was the creation of social conditions which would allow the instinctive desire for a family to be sufficiently met. These ranged from income tax relief to more nursery provision, from improved house design to increased access to labour-saving devices.

Similar proposals and more were contained in the 1942 Beveridge Report which heralded the introduction of the modern welfare state. Again eugenicist notions provided the context for some of the policies advocated. Children's Allowances (now Child Benefit) were recommended not only to guarantee a minimum income and to ensure that unemployment benefit did not exceed the earnings of those in work, but to encourage population growth:

> With its present rate of reproduction, the British race cannot continue: means of reversing the recent course of the birthrate must be found . . . children's allowances can help to restore the birthrate, both by making it possible for parents who desire more children to bring them into the world without damaging the chances of those already born, and as a signal of the national

interest in children, setting the tone of public opinion. (Beveridge 1942: 154)

The Family Allowances Act was passed by the 1945 coalition government. Benefit was paid directly to the mother on the birth of her second child. A survey of hospital patients in 1946 found that nearly all the women interviewed believed that family allowances had been introduced to boost the birth rate rather than to alleviate their hardships (Riley 1981: 94).

One possible 'solution' to the so-called 'population problem' that was firmly ruled out by the British state was encouraging immigration to Britain by the non-Anglo-Saxon inhabitants of the British colonies. This was in spite of the fact that official concern about population *growth* in some of the colonies was being expressed at this time. A 1945 Royal Commission on social conditions in the West Indies recommended the establishment of birth control clinics and there was growing support among British administrators in India for measures to curb the birth rate (Smith 1973).

The crudest of eugenicist reasons were used to rule out immigration to Britain to boost the British population. The 1949 Royal Commission on Population declared that such immigration would:

> Involve serious problems of assimilation beyond those of training and housing. Immigration on a large scale into a fully established society like ours could only be welcomed without reserve if the immigrants were of good human stock and were not prevented by their religion or race from intermarrying with the host population and becoming merged in it . . . there is little or no prospect that we should be able to apply these conditions to large scale immigration in the future. (Royal Commission on Population 1949: ch.2)

THE BABY BOOM AND RACIST POPULATION CONTROLS

After the decline in the birth rate had reached its peak in 1933, there was a rapid rise from 1941 onwards culminating in the 'baby boom' of the mid-1950s to the mid-1960s. In 1976 it was projected by the government's actuary department that the UK population would increase by a further 15 million by the year 2000, to reach over 70 million. This led to a flurry of activity in official quarters. The Labour government under Harold Wilson set up an unpublicised committee of senior civil servants to advise the government on how to control

Britain's population growth. There were plans afoot to establish a central population unit in the Cabinet Ofice, but Labour lost power to the Tories before this could be implemented. Then in response to a resolution signed by more than 300 MPs, the new Select Committee on Science and Technology initiated an enquiry into population growth, which reported in 1971.

While the prime focus of the national attention on population growth may well have been the future *size* of British population, it is clear that concerns about the *composition* of that population were also pronounced. The cruder aspects of eugenics were completely discredited by the social democratic consensus which dominated the British state in the 1960s and 1970s. But, although largely unacknowledged, such ideas clearly lay behind the development of immigration controls to curb the entry of black British subjects to the UK in those decades.

The justification given by successive governments for this legislation was population growth. The problem, so the argument ran, was not one of inferior stock or even of cultural incompatibility but of too many people competing for too few resources in an overcrowded island. This was frequently the kind of position adopted by Labour Party leaders in the 1960s and 1970s. It was not that they themselves were racist, they would protest. They were opposed to racial discrimination and passed laws against it. They were simply responding to the will and anxieties of the people! In 1967 Prime Minister Harold Wilson approached former Tory minister David Renton about studies that the Labour government had initiated into the policy implications of an increased population. He wrote in a letter: 'if any of these implications appeared to be intolerable we could then consider what needed to be done' (Select Committee on Science and Technology 1971). The following year the Labour government introduced the 1968 Commonwealth Immigrants Act to stop British Asians living in East Africa from being automatically entitled to come to Britain. The Act was passed amidst fears that large numbers of British Asians were on the point of taking up their right to live in the UK, due to expulsions and persecution in some East African countries. It did not prevent *all* immigration – only immigration by those without British *ancestry*.

Again the 1971 Immigration Act was introduced by Edward Heath's Conservative government in the same year that the Select Committee on Population Policy produced its first report. Among other things it noted that 'the fertility rate of the immigrants in this country is . . . slightly higher than the British characteristic average'. It urged the government to 'act to prevent the consequences of population growth becoming intolerable for the every day conditions of life', and proposed that a special government office be set up to study and advise on population policy. Among its remit would be 'internal and external migration and consequences' (Select Committee on Science and Technology 1971). The all-party committee was very disappointed when the government refused to act on its recommendation to set up a permanent office. But the new Immigration Act showed that the government was indeed concerned to curb population growth, not by the population as a whole, but by 'non-patrials', i.e. black UK citizens. The year after the new Act was passed the same government took Britain into the EEC, opening the door to whoever wished to seek work in the UK – provided they were European![5]

The drift of post-1971 immigration policy has been almost entirely devoted to separating black families so as to keep the size of the black British population tightly controlled. This has chiefly been achieved by constructing women as wives and mothers or 'dependants', much as in pre-1981 nationality legislation. Whilst, until recently, theoretically entitled to follow their husbands wherever they may live (a right much more easily exercised if their husbands happen to be white), women – including those born in the UK – have not even been given a paper right to bring over foreign-born husbands to live with them.[6] Legally defined as 'dependants', they of course cannot be married and bring over 'dependants' of their own. As former Home Secretary William Whitelaw put it in a speech to the Central Council of the Conservative Party in 1978: 'it surely cannot be unreasonable to argue that in accordance with the customs of Europe and the Indian subcontinent, the abode of the husband in a marriage should normally be viewed as the natural place of residence of the family' (speech distributed by the Conservative central office).

In practice this policy has been used almost exclusively to prevent *black* women from bringing over husbands from abroad and, in particular, to prevent Asian women from engaging in 'arranged marriages' with men from the Indian sub-continent. Even where the Home Office acknowledges a marriage is 'genuine', the couple have to have met before the marriage and 'prove' that the 'primary purpose' of their marriage was not immigration, before they are allowed to settle in Britain.

When the European Court ruled in 1985 that British immigration law discriminated against women, the government responded to this binding judgement by reducing the rights of men to those of women. Had they not done this, of course, more black families would have been united with the concomitant growth in the black population of Britain.

The 1970s was also the period in which the government started to collect statistics to gauge the size of the black, rather than just the immigrant, population. A question on the birthplace of respondents has been asked since the 1841 census. But in 1971 a question was introduced to the census on birthplace of parents to estimate the number of people from the 'New Commonwealth' (that is, all Commonwealth countries *excluding* Australia, Canada and New Zealand) living in Britain, including those who were themselves born in the UK.[7] Two years previously the birthplace of parents started to be recorded on birth certificates for the first time and the birthplace of the deceased was marked on death certificates. By combining all this information, together with figures on net immigration, the government is able to produce annual published estimates of the 'New Commonwealth' population as well as figures of the 'New Commonwealth' birth rate. Successive governments have justified counting the black population of Britain on the grounds that it is necessary for devising social policies to deal with the discrimination and 'disadvantage' they face. But it is difficult not to share the scepticism of black groups who ask how many times they need to be counted before such policies are forthcoming. However sincere those in the 'liberal lobby' may be in insisting that such statistics are put to beneficial use, their significance is not lost on sections of the media or some Tory MPs. For them these statistics are a way of gauging the British stock – a means of assessing what proportion of the British population is black and what proportion is 'truly British'. Articles in the press reflect this preoccupation. And not just the 'popular' press: 'immigrant mothers lead baby league' was the headline of an article in *The Times* (14 September 1985) following publication of the latest statistics on births to parents from the 'New Commonwealth'. 'More than half the births in four London boroughs last year were to mothers born outside the UK', the story read. Likewise Tory MPs such as Tony Marlow (and the now deposed Harvey Proctor) have used the opportunity of the annual head-count of the black population to publicise dire warnings about the future awaiting Britain. 'This country is being progressively colonised', Marlow stated on one such occasion. 'It is a peaceful invasion but one which threatens to destroy our heritage and our traditions' (*Daily Mail*, 9 April 1982).

The preoccupation with *who* comes in has also affected eligibility for benefits under the modern welfare state, much as in the early part of this century. As discussed earlier, one of the main factors involved in shaping British social policy has been the production of a physically fit nation capable of carrying out its responsibilities in the world. The belief that the health of the nation equals the wealth of the nation is now so widely accepted as to be unquestioned. And hand in hand with this assumption has been the conviction that the benefits of the welfare state are for the British only – foreigners keep out!

In fact when the postwar welfare state was first created mere presence in the UK was sufficient for entitlement to national assistance and to health treatment. But this soon changed. Following parliamentary pressure the 1949 National Health Service Act empowered the Minister of Health to make regulations to exclude from free treatment people who were not 'ordinarily resident' in the UK. Numerous government circulars were issued over the years underlining who was ineligible for free care until regulations tying hospital treatment under the NHS to residency tests were enacted in 1982.

Under the 1971 Immigration Act, all non-patrial 'dependants' seeking admission had to prove that they would not have 'recourse to public funds'.[8] Now 'dependants' who are not British citizens are placed in the same situation. Under the 1980 Social Security Act 'sponsors' can be charged with a criminal offence if they refuse to maintain a 'dependant' relative whom they have brought over. There is no time limit, in theory at least, on this liability. Whether they come for a short period or are permanent residents, non-naturalised 'dependants' are deemed second-class citizens, ineligible for the benefits they pay for in taxes. Under the new Tory Immigration Bill these restrictions will be extended to apply to the 'dependants' of those who settled in the UK *before* the 1971 Immigration Act was introduced in 1973. Families who have been divided for years, often because of delays and obstacles in immigration procedures, will now remain divided because the original settler, who will have been paying taxes for 15 years or more, will be forced to maintain and accommodate the entire family without access to public funds or state housing.

It must be said, however, that although successive British governments have engineered a wide range of social and immigration policies in an attempt to get the 'population mix' right, they have never interfered *directly* in the national birth rate. In a Council of Europe paper published in 1981, Britain was one of 12 countries which was described as having no policy of direct intervention in the national fertility rate.[9] While there were prosecutions of birth control advocates in the late nineteenth and early twentieth centuries, birth control itself has never been strictly illegal in Britain. Similarly, although family allowances, along with other social policies, were partly introduced to render child-bearing less burdensome and thereby increase the birth rate, modern child benefits were *not* withdrawn in the period when fears of a population explosion were at their greatest.

It could be argued that the introduction in 1967 of widely available contraceptive advice and of abortion on 'social' as well as medical grounds did come about when concern over population growth was at its peak. The official rationale for introducing such measures was to increase the choice of the individual. Given the extent of popular support for contraception and abortion, this probably was the major factor involved. The attention paid to the birth rate at the time was arguably no more than an additional conducive factor.

Testimonies from black women, however, have provided disturbing evidence that they receive greater encouragement from some sections of the National Service to have abortions or sterilisation in the face of unplanned pregnancies than white women do. This issue became sufficiently significant to split the National Abortion Campaign in 1983. The Reproductive Rights Campaign was formed to reflect the fact that for all women to have 'the right to choose' how to control their own fertility there needed to be a movement which catered for the conflicting pressures faced by black and white women. If white women argued that they were denied the freedom of choice *not* to breed, too often black women complained that they were prevented from deciding *to have* children when they wished to (Bryan *et al*. 1985: 100–10).

Similarly, it has been alleged that Asian women, in particular, have been more liable to receive the injectable contraceptive, Depo Provera, than white women. This is a particularly reliable form of birth control but one whose attendant health risks are said by some contraceptive specialists to be very high.[10] This is not to imply that there is a eugenicist-inspired state conspiracy to prevent black women from having children. It is to suggest that the official attention paid to the black birth rate, even though it is alleged to be for purely benign reasons, has permeated into the general consciousness. As a result it seems that some medical workers act out of their own initiative to encourage black women to terminate unplanned pregnancies and to use any method available to avoid them in the future. In some cases, no doubt, there are health workers who do not even require the state to encourage them to take preemptive action to control the black birth rate.

CONCLUSIONS

In the construction of the modern British nation the role of women has been crucial. As it is assumed that nationality is something transmitted by birth, it is women, of course, who physically reproduce the nation, as any strategy for limiting the boundaries of a nation to a particular people has recognised. However, in spite of periodic panics over projections of a declining or exploding British population – for example, in the 1930s or 1960s – there has been no concerted state plan to directly control the birth rate (although there has been evidence of independent coercion by health workers on black women to control their fertility). Neither has a policy of repatriation been introduced in modern Britian, although there have been cases of this in the past,[11] and the threat that the government will be pushed down this path by pressure from the far right, in and outside the Tory party, has never disappeared.

At the same time – drawing on the persisting myth of a continuous lineage of white Anglo-Saxons with exclusive rights to the benefits of Britain – the British Isles *have* been largely reserved for the white British, with black Britons and those defined as 'aliens' kept out. This has mainly been achieved through a deliberate immigration policy pursued by successive British governments.[12] Policies implemented for a variety of purposes, such as the introduction of family allowances, have also contributed by helping to boost the quality and quantity of white Britons. Whilst it is always possible to invent conspiracy theories, there are historical developments which occur through deliberate state planning. Keeping Britain for the white British has been one of them!

And what of the future? If the majority grouping within the state continues to see Britain's best interests as lying within the EEC – and the current trend of British capitalism suggests they will – then the British national identity, which the right in particular tenaciously hangs on to, may gradually be superceded by a European one. The freedom of movement granted to European workers in the early 1970s, compared with the barriers put in the way of non-patrial British workers, marked the possible beginning of this process. The introduction of a European passport, bitterly resented by the far right, may prove to be the next. From an internationalist perspective the move from narrow Englander to pan-Europeanism may well act to offset the most inward-looking aspects of traditional British nationalism. But there is no guarantee that some of the crudest racist and eugenicist notions will be relinquished in this development, nor that policies to encourage women to reproduce will fade into history. In April 1984 the European Parliament called for 'concerted action' to reverse the 'drastic decline' of the Community's birth rate. The parliament was told that the population of the member states would drop from 8.8 per cent of the world's total in 1950 to 4.5 per cent by the year 2000, and a presidency paper on the subject warned: 'a nation without enough children would be a sad nation. The same applies to Europe as a whole' (*Guardian*, 13 April 1984). With some European countries, notably France and Germany, expelling their 'guest workers' as unemployment sets in, there is little reason to hope that any European nation of the future will be less racist than the British nation of the past.

NOTES

1. Legally speaking the category of British citizen was not created until the 1981 British Nationality Act came into force in 1983. Until then the term 'British subject' was used to denote roughly what we now understand by British citizen.
2. Under this Act, passed by the postwar Labour government, all citizens of Commonwealth countries, whether independent or not, continued to be 'British subjects'. As such they, along with Irish citizens, were not subject to British immigration control (until 1962) and were granted full civic rights if resident in Britain. Broadly speaking, those born in independent ex-colonies also became citizens of their new countries, whilst those born in Britain and any of the remaining colonies became citizens of the UK and colonies.
3. Patrials were *either* UK citizens who were born or adopted or registered or naturalised or resident for five years or more in the UK *or else* they were Commonwealth citizens with a British-born parent *or* a Commonwealth wife of a patrial man. Under the Immigration Rules for administering the Act, Commonwealth citizens with a British-born grandparent

were, and are, also entitled to live in the UK indefinitely. Clearly unless a black UK citizen was actually born in Britain or had lived there for more than five years, they were unlikely to be patrial whereas few white Commonwealth citizens, whether or not born or living in Britain and whether or not UK citizens, were unlikely to be 'caught out' by the patriality clause because of their ancestry.

4. BDTCs are only entitled to live in the colony they already inhabit. BOCs, mainly Asians living in East Africa, are not *entitled* to live anywhere, as a result of this status, and have to queue for discretionary vouchers to live in the UK.

5. Under EEC law nationals of other EEC member states are granted a residence permit provided they find work in the UK within six months.

6. Although wives of men settled here have had an entitlement to join them which has been denied to husbands and women settled here, in practice thousands of wives and children have been refused entry each year since 1973. A paper given by Home Office civil servants in 1983, leaked to the *Guardian* in April 1985, revealed that long queues for entry to Britain by families in the Indian sub-continent are maintained as the 'primary regulator' of immigration from that part of the world.

7. In the 1981 census this question was altered to 'birthplace of head of household'. Using statistical formulae the black population as a whole is calculated on this basis.

8. Unless they were the wives or minor children of Commonwealth men settled in the UK before the 1971 Act came into force, in which case they had an absolute right of entry.

9. The member states which were reported to have interventionist fertility policies were France, Greece, Liechtenstein and Luxembourg. Out of 20 states, nine expressed concern over their country's birth rate because they considered it to be too low.

10. A report by obstetrician Wendy Savage, 'The Use of Dep Provera in East London' in *Fertility and Contraception*, vol. 12, no. 3 (July 1978), showed that this contraceptive is administered in hospitals with a large proportion of Asian women patients. It did not conclusively demonstrate, therefore, that Asian women are generally more likely to be given Depo Provera and, to my knowledge, no such study has yet been conducted.

11. *Examples* include the expulsion of all Jews from England in 1290; the removal of some 'Black Moors' from Elizabethan England; legislation permitting the deportation of destitute Indian seamen in the 1890s, despite their British subject status; and the repatriation of hundreds of black people following the 1919 anti-black riots in Liverpool and Cardiff.

12. This is despite the fact that the demographic estimates of the late 1960s have proved to be grossly exaggerated. The UK population is expected to rise by less than a million by the end of the century. There was almost no population growth between 1971 and 1981 with the birth rate reaching a new low in 1977. Moreover, it is predicted that the annual net outflow of people from the UK will be 31 000 on average until the

end of the century (Hubbak 1983). This is in keeping with the past. Other than in the late 1950s and early 1960s emigration has exceeded immigration to Britain virtually every year since British settlers started migrating to the colonies from the 1820s onwards.

BIBLIOGRAPHY

Barker, Martin (1981) *The New Racism: Conservatives and the Ideology of the Tribe* (London: Junction Books).

Beveridge, William (1942) *Social Insurance and Allied Services*, CMND 4606 (London: HMSO).

Bryan, B., S. Dudzi & S. Scafe (1985) *The Heart of the Race: Black Women's Lives in Britain* (London: Virago).

Cohen, Steve (1985) 'Anti-semitism, Immigration Controls and the Welfare State', *Critical Social Policy* (Summer).

Council of Europe (1981) *Population Policies in the Member States of the Council of Europe*, CDDE (81) 6.

Dale, Jenny & Peggy Foster (1986) *Feminists and State Welfare* (London: Routledge & Kegan Paul), 73–92.

Davin, Anna (1978) 'Immigration and Motherhood', *History Workshop*, 9–52.

Fraser, D. (1975) *The Evolution of the British Welfare State* (London: Macmillan).

Fryer, Peter (1984) *Staying Power: the History of Black People in Britain* (London: Pluto).

Gordon, Paul & Francesca Klug (1986) *New Right, New Racism* (London: Searchlight).

Gordon, Paul & Anne Newnham (1985) *Passport to Benefits: Racism in Social Security* (London: Runnymede Trust/CPAG).

Hubbak, David (1983) *Population Trends in Great Britain* (London: Simon Population Trust/Policy Studies Institute).

Nairn, Tom (1977) *The Break up of Britain* (London: Verso).

Riley, Denise (1981) 'The Free Mothers: Pronatalism and Working Mothers in Industry at the End of the Last War in Britain', *History Workshop*, 11 (Spring).

Rowbotham, Sheila (1973) *Hidden from History* (London: Pluto).

Royal Commission on Population (1949) *Report*, CMND 7695 (London: HMSO).

Select Committee on Science and Technology (1971) *Population of the UK*, H.C. 379 (London: HMSO).

Semmel, Bernard (1960) *Immigration and Social Reform: English Social Imperial Thought 1895–1914* (London: George Allen & Unwin).

Smith, T.D. (1973) *The Politics of Family Planning in the Third World* (London: Allen & Unwin).

West Indian Royal Commission (1945) *Report*, CMND 6607 (London: HMSO).

Whitelaw, W. (1988) *Speech to the Central Council of the Conservative Party* (Conservative Central Office).

WING – Women, Immigration and Nationality Group (1985) *Worlds Apart: Women under Immigration and Nationality Law* (London: Pluto).

3 Women, Nation and the State in Australia
Marie de Lepervanche

INTRODUCTION

In Australia's multi-cultural society of the 1980s both state and federal legislation outlaws race and gender discrimination. Even so, Australia's major political, legal and educational institutions, as well as many social customs, are derived from British liberal democratic models which privilege British over non-British and male over female. Women also remain affected by the class structure and ethnic/racial mix present-day Australia and by the legacy of social practices that had their origin in the formation of a 'white' Australian nation. In the move towards federation of the colonies, accomplished in 1901, racist practices against Aboriginals, Asian and Melanesian immigrants, legitimated by 'scientific' notions of biological differences, helped weld the 'white' nation. Only in the 1970s was the 'white' Australia policy finally abandoned, together with the abandonment of a policy which had enjoined immigrants and Aboriginals to assimilate to Anglo conformity. Since 1973 public policy has emphasised the celebration of ethnicity, yet despite the multi-cultural rhetoric some nationalisms are more acceptable than others.

The chapter is going to look at the history of ethnic/racial divisions in Australia as have been constructed by the Australian state, and at the specific roles women played in these processes. In particular it is going to look at women as the 'breeders of the white race'.

EARLY ETHNIC/RACIAL DIVISIONS

From the days of first white settlement until the end of the Second World War the ethnic composition of the white population was always heavily Anglo-Celtic. Even so, colonial settlers were often troubled by race differences which set whites apart from the indigenous Aboriginals in the first place and later from Indian indentured labourers, Chinese gold diggers, Afghan cameleers and Melanesian cane workers. By the end of the last century Australians had clearly distinguished themselves and the acceptable white Europeans from undesirable (predominantly Mediterranean) Europeans and non-Europeans. Yet, even among the British, class, ethnic and gender divisions affected people's lives differently. From colonial times until comparatively recently a distinct cultural division between Protestant British and (Irish) Roman Catholic coloured Australian social life. In the nineteenth century the Catholic Irish working class component of the population contributed substantially to the development of the Australian Labour movement, while the colonial establishments remained attached to all things British and Protestant. But, despite their 'ethnic' disadvantages, Irish Catholics were never excluded from Australian society as much as Aboriginals and Asian immigrants were. White settlement deprived the Aboriginal people of their land, and colonial, state and federal legislation restricted their residence, their right to vote, their employment, freedom of movement, their marriages and the custody, care and education of their children. While white British settlers were encouraged to establish their families and populate the land, Aboriginal family life was disrupted or destroyed. Legislation concerning 'half castes' even determined who was and was not Aboriginal and who did and did not receive pensions. Only during the 1960s were Aboriginals enfranchised and counted in the federal census. Although modified land rights and anti-discrimination legislation exists today, the extent of white racism can be gauged by the continuing high rates of Aboriginal infant and child mortality, in their shorter life expectancy, their high unemployment figures, poor health and educational disadvantages and in their over-representation in prison statistics. The contact experience for Aboriginal women also included sexual as well as other forms of exploitation by whites (Grimshaw 1981).

Asians and Melanesians were introduced to the colonies in the last century as indentured labour for pastoral and plantation properties. After gold was discovered in the 1850s, free Chinese also arrived and competition for gold brought hostile reactions from Europeans. These Asian and Island immigrations were predominantly male. Not only were whites frightened that the 'lower races' might breed if coloured women entered but, as Saunders comments, those Pacific Island women who did enter, and whose menfolk provided the Kanaka (indentured Melanesian) labour in Queensland's sugar fields, were not themselves acceptable initially as indentured servants 'because their reproductive capacities could endanger the whole structure of an easily replaceable, fluid, servile labour force' (1982: 32). Colonial and later state legislation inhibited Asian settlement and activity, and with federation in 1901 the Immigration Restriction Act (otherwise known as the 'white' Australian policy) was passed, which impeded Asian immigration until the 1960s.

Before the Second World War a number of northern and Mediterranean Europeans had established the nucleus of later 'ethnic' settlements. Even so, their entry was restricted during the 1920s and some southern Europeans were even categorised as non-white (Evans *et al.* 1975: 6). During the 1930s, refugees from Hitler were also regarded with suspicion, especially by trade unionists. Many pre-war immigrant men started small businesses and their wives and daughters, if present, usually contributed to the family enterprise, although their labour was frequently unpaid (Martin 1984).

IMMIGRANT ETHNIC AND GENDER VARIETY

Immediately after the Second World War immigrant programmes were explicitly linked with measures to exclude the 'yellow hordes' to the north and to maintain the white British character of the 'race' within. The Pacific war had increased anxieties about defence and, together with a need for labour power, this prompted the massive postwar immigration programme. Compared with the pre-war predominantly male immigrations, the postwar programme favoured a more balanced sex ratio, and the newcomers were expected to enter the urban industrial labour force rather than agricultural work.

By the 1960s the British emphasis had become diluted as the demand for labourers forced Australia to seek immigrants from non-British and eventually non-European sources. The 'white' Australia policy was liberalised to permit the entry of professionally or technically qualified Asians and their dependants. But unlike New Commonwealth immigrants in the UK who have entered the industrial working class, the postwar Asian settlers have tended to occupy petit bourgeois or middle class positions and do not constitute 'problems', although in recent years some racist hostility has erupted againt Vietnamese refugees, many of whom hold working class jobs.

By the 1980s Australia had received more than 3 million immigrants from more than 60 nations. Only in Israel has immigration had a greater relative impact on the composition of the population, workforce and social life in general (Collins 1984: 8). In 1947 most

Australians in the workforce were Anglo-Celtic and male: only one-fifth of the total workforce was female. By 1981, 37 per cent of employed persons were female and the workforce in general was more immigrant in origin and less Anglophone (Collins 1984: 11).

Among OECD (Organisation for Economic Co-operation and Development) nations Australia has one of the most sex-segregated labour markets by occupation and superimposed on these divisions are differences of ethnic origin: ideologies of sexism and racism sustain these distinctions (Power 1975). In 1971 where 55.9 per cent of Greek-born and 54.7 per cent of Yugoslavian-born women were employed as process workers and labourers, only 9.3 per cent of Australian-born women were. In 1984 63 per cent of female employees were concentrated in clerical, sales and service occupations: others (and particularly Mediterraneans) were in manufacturing jobs (Collins 1984). This kind of ethnic and sex segmentation disadvantages immigrant women particularly: their conditions are poor, their health suffers and they are liable to stereotyping as 'naturally' stupid and suited to boring, repetitive work.

Postwar immigration to Australia was initially accompanied by the publicly sanctioned policy of assimilation to Anglo conformity, in force until the early 1970s even after Australia had begun to recruit labour from the Middle East and Asia. As late as 1968 the Minister for Immigration was quoted as saying 'We must have a single culture.'

For a while the non-British were referred to as 'national groups' but during the 1970s they became transformed into 'ethnic groups' after Labour came to power in 1973 and multi-culturalism became government policy. Behind this acceptance of cultural variety there was, first, the settlement of more non-British than ever before in Australian history. Second, many of these newcomers had begun to demand a voice in social affairs, had the vote and were critical of assimilation policy. Third, a number of Australians shared these sentiments and were increasingly critical of some problems immigrant assimilation entailed; and a poverty survey of Melbourne had shown that 16.2 per cent of Greeks and 15.3 per cent of Italians were below the poverty line compared with 7.7 per cent of the total population who were below this income level. By the mid-1970s public response had apparently undergone a complete metamorphosis: the new emphasis was on cultural diversity. Newcomers were invited to celebrate their ethnicity and the rhetoric of assimilation was formally abandoned (cf. de Lepervanche 1980).

CITIZENS, PERMANENT RESIDENTS AND FAMILY REUNIONS

Australia does not sanction the introduction of guest workers. Immigrants are expected to apply for permanent residence and eventually become citizens. In 1948 the Nationality and Citizenship Act first defined Australian citizenship; before then Australians were British subjects, like others in the Commonwealth. Amendments to the Citizenship Act in 1973 removed some of the anomalies with respect to citizenship which had previously discriminated against non-European British subjects, and in that year non-European immigrants first became eligible for assisted passages which had previously been available only to white British and some selected European settlers.

To produce citizens, the family reunion provisions have constituted important planks of immigration policy. Initally defined in 1947 to include extended family members, the term 'family reunion' has since contracted and expanded in meaning. When assimilation ideology gave way to multi-culturalism in the 1970s, for example, the ideal family was the nuclear mode, and working immigrant women often 'failed' to conform. After ethnic pressure for liberalising family reunion provisions, concessions were made in 1982 with respect to adult brothers and sisters and adult children, although new guidelines in July 1985 stressed the *immediate* family (spouses, dependent children and aged parents) rather than the extended unit. Special provisions are available for introducing fiancé(e)s.

The stress on women as producers of families goes back a long way, despite a number of nineteenth-century male immigrations. The first assisted immigrants to this country were 50 women from Cork who arrived in 1831. They were expected to:

> exert a sobering influence over the moral debauchery held to be rampant in the colony as a result of the excess of single men; they were to become the wives of labouring men and the mothers of their children and they were to provide menial domestic (later factory) labour in the homes and industries of the colonial elite . . .
> [Later] preference in assistance was given to young married couples, their children and to single women between eighteen and thirty years who came to the colony under the protection of a married couple. Thus, the ideal female immigrant had . . . to . . .

be *dependent* on the patronage of some form of male-headed household. (Martin 1984: 109)

Some women have migrated independently, but since 1945 most women and especially non-English-speaking female settlers have been dependants of men. In official eyes they have been expected to establish and/or maintain family units and relations in the interests of anchoring their male compatriots emotionally, and to provide consumption units for Australia's expanding capitalism. But their experiences in this country do not conform neatly to the planners' tidy sexual division of labour. Among new female arrivals, workforce participation high, between 50 per cent and 85 per cent in the decade 1970–80 (Martin 1984: 112). Without the customary support of kin and neighbours available in their homelands, many of these women see their lives torn between jobs and children. Together with Australian-born women, they are also the victims of grossly inadequate childcare.

Some of the (male) experts on the family in the 1960s saw immigrants, and especially women, as 'problems' because their supposed seclusion within family life impeded their assimilation. Others feared that children of working mothers were disadvantaged, although one expert considered a more liberal resolution to the contradictions women experienced: 'We must beware of drawing false conclusions about the results of . . . employment on the home life and upbringing of immigrant children . . . many wives assist . . . in running a cafe or small store . . . they are therefore "at home" when the children return from school' (Price 1966: 18–19).

As Martin has noted, most analyses of immigration tend to see production as male enterprise and consumption and population growth within the family as female responsibilities. Thus the 'ideological division of our world into masculine and feminine spheres, corresponding to a production/consumption split, is reproduced in migration policy and has governed female migration to Australia' (1984: 111). This ideological divide has indeed been a fundamental tenet of white Anglo male hegemony in Australia, and the social construction of women as dependent breeders has been oppressive for all women. But for those immigrant women who have endured extreme exploitation in their paid work, as well as subordination in the domestic sphere, the oppression has been particularly acute. Yet these kinds of variation in women's experience are not always recognised. In more ways than one, women tend to be severely stereotyped in male discourse or absent from it altogether as the following material illustrates.

BREEDERS OF THE WHITE RACE

The traditional sexual division of labour in the domestic sphere and workplace has been continually sanctioned in portrayals of the Australian way of life and national character, which have invariably been by white men. Until well into the 1950s the 'typical Australian' was a white man with British forbears; he came from the bush and practised mateship. A second type of Australian identity emerged in the 1960s: although still male, Anglo-Celtic and white, he was no longer from the bush but thoroughly middle class and suburban. By the 1970s when we were urged by the state to celebrate the different ethnic backgrounds of postwar immigrants, the Australian national character transformed into a number of versions. One was multi-cultural and supposedly sophisticated, while another remained distinctly 'ocker' and male (cf. Oxley 1979: 193). Throughout this literature, if women did appear they were white, English speakers associated with domestic life where they remained rather dumb, even dangerous, greedy or distracting the men from carrying out their important tasks (cf. Horne 1972: 193; Conway 1978: 25).

Without the vote until 1902, women were conspicuously absent from parliamentary decision-making at federation; they were in 'the home' as objects of 'protection', particularly from those not eligible for inclusion in the new nation, namely the male non-white immigrants from Asia and the Pacific who were permitted domicile or eventually excluded by the 'white' Australia policy. According to clergymen, politicians and journalists, the black and yellow men had posed a threat to virtuous white women. As the *Queensland Evangelical Standard* put it in 1876:

The Asiatics were not children but savages, with irrepressible savage natures of a kind most dangerous to the safety of unprotected females . . . What happiness can any poor foolish country woman of ours expect from uniting in marriage with soft, pulpy, childish but passionate kanaka or the lithe, yellow-skinned mummy of the Celestial Empire? (quoted in Evans *et al.* 1975: 262)

The Asiatic 'threat' was not the only one: the Australian birth-rate fell from 38 per 1000 to 27 per 1000 in 1900, which caused alarm in government circles as policy was geared to increasing the country's (white) population. Explanations for the falling birth-rate included the use of contraceptives which were allegedly contributing to 'race suicide'. In New South Wales a report by the Commonwealth Statistician noted that the limitation of family size was a selfish and decadent phenomenon. The advertising of contraceptives was made illegal (McQueen 1978: 60). One of the Birth Rate Commissioners in 1903 labelled the women's rights movements a 'formidable adversary to fecundity' (quoted in Bacchi 1980: 148), and a lecturer in physiology at Melbourne University, attacking the emancipation of women for the decline in the birth rate concluded, in his presidential address to the Australasian Association for the Advancement of Science in 1901:

> The propagation of the Anglo-Saxon race has been placed largely under voluntary control, owing to the education of women. The extent to which this control is resorted to may determine the fate of the Empire . . . it is not possible to cheat God Almighty without paying a very heavy penalty both personally and racially. (Quoted in Bacchi 1980: 149)

Although by 1910, one-fifth of the workforce was female and many others worked (and still do) in material production on farms and in small businesses for which they are not paid and for which they get no public recognition as workers, it was widely accepted that a woman's job was to care for her husband and children. Justice Higgins 'Harvester' Judgement of 1907 had even instituted a policy which sanctioned by law the existing practices of sex segregation in social life: he introduced the notion of a 'living' wage sufficient to keep a man, his wife and three children (Baldock 1983: 34). All unskilled male workers were to receive this basic wage, despite the fact that 45 per cent of the male workforce was single at the time of the judgement. There was no basic wage established for women, and in 1912 Justice Higgins instituted separate pay rates for women's work without any regard for productivity: women were to get a male rate if they did 'men's work' and competed with men, but if they did 'women's work' they were paid a woman's (lower) wage. The judgement deemed that the 'normal needs' of men were greater than

women's, as men had to support the family whereas women supported only themselves. Curiously, a survey in 1928 showed that 30 per
cent of women were partially or wholly supporting other family
members (Cass 1983: 62).

Simultaneously as white women were encouraged to be home-
makers, the rapid urban expansion of the late nineteenth century
generated concern for health and sanitation as much as for families,
and advice through health agencies and public lectures was continually directed at women. In Melbourne working class suburbs,
'Meetings for Wives and Daughters' were held to 'secure the
co-operation of the home-ruler, be she mother, wife or daughter, by
interesting her personally in the work of sanitary reform' (Reiger
1982: 75). There were very few non-European women in Australia at
this time, except for Aboriginals and they tended to be herded into
reserves or left to their own devices in the bush or on the edges of
country towns. Older Aboriginal women, particularly, struggled to
keep their families together while they endured severe ill-health, low
life expectancy, high infant and child mortality rates and harassment
by white (usually male) officials, which often led to 'the institutionali-
sation of the young and the sexual exploitation of girls resulting in
illegitimate births' (Grimshaw 1981: 91). High rates of male unemployment, the absence of their menfolk as itinerant labour and their
heavy drinking did not make the women's lives any easier (Grimshaw
1981).

The domestic labour and much of the breeding that engaged white
women during the last years of the nineteenth century provided the
grim fodder for the slaughter at Gallipoli and in France between 1914
and 1918. Over 330 770 men went overseas and 63 163, or nearly one
in five, died on active service. Only one in three escaped wounds,
capture or death (Gammage 1975: 283).

Women are conspicuously absent from the war histories except in
so far as they served as nurses, did war work or 'gave in sacrifice' their
sons, husbands and lovers for the 'noble' cause. Moreover, the
constructive enterprise of giving birth during these war years was
accorded solely to the men: the disaster at Gallipoli even became the
'birthplace' of Australian nationhood (Bean 1981).

Women had not entered the workforce in vast numbers during the
First World War. Where they were in paid employment before and
after the war their jobs were concentrated in 'female' industries, such
as domestic service and clothing factories (Power 1975: 229). Until
1942 their minimum wage was 54 per cent that for male workers

(Baldock 1983: 26). These circumstances weakened their potential for general political or industrial activity. The feminist agitation that did occur centred on matters of citizenship and suffrage and on women's ability to bear children. Before and after getting the vote in 1902, women had 'campaigned for legal reforms on the issues which *they* perceived as significant: the social injustices and exploitations of women and children' (Allen 1979: 107). In stressing their differences from men as the basis of their demands for citizen rights, women even attracted some converts from the patriarchal establishment to support them in the years 1891–1901. Most of these politically active women were middle class and in the years preceding the First World War the issues that received parliamentary sponsorship were those supporting middle class concepts of childhood and family life. But even these activities were not always successful. In debates in the New South Wales parliament over the Bill to raise the age of consent from 14 to 16, members denounced the measures as an 'intolerable interference with the liberty of men and as a contravention of nature: in a sub-tropical climate, it was said, girls ripened into women earlier than in England' (Allen 1979: 111).

Before the First World War the only Commonwealth provision to recognise women independently as citizens with sex-specific claims was the universalist maternity allowance of 1912 from which Aboriginal and Asian women were excluded (Roe 1983: 7). The accent on white children populating the nation emerged again in debates on child endowment in the 1920s. Associated with wage fixation legislation, child endowment (paid to wives) was introduced by New South Wales, for example, in 1927. In arguing for the benefit, women maintained that there was no guarantee that husbands would share their 'living' wage equitably with their wives and children, and emphasised the contribution of women's domestic labour, the recognition of their rights and their children's to a separate income, as well as the necessity of supplementing the 'living' wage itself. They also saw endowment as a precondition for equal pay (Cass 1983a: 56–64). Men's arguments revolved around a clash of class interests that saw Labour stress the 'living' wage and its need for supplementation, while Conservatives, worried about profits and the possibility of the provision to mothers threatening the conjugal relationship and male authority, stressed the notion of the 'capacity of industry to pay' (Cass 1983: 55). Male concerns with 'race suicide' if women did not perform their 'natural' duty also surfaced. The New South Wales Minister for Public Health and Motherhood, in his support for welfare, complained:

the black races are breeding ten to one of the white races. The civilised races are being over educated. Women try to avoid the hardship of bearing and breeding children. They want to enjoy life and the bearing of children is looked upon as an encumbrance and a hindrance . . . The only way to alter the balance in favour of the white races is to ensure that the women who are prepared to do their duty should not be penalised, as is the case today. (New South Wales Parliamentary Debates 1920: 4087, quoted in Cass 1983a: 68–9)

It is sobering to remember that the maternal mortality rate in Australia actually rose between 1910 and 1930. In the 1920s it accounted for one-sixth of deaths of married women in early and mid-adult life (Roe 1983: 10).

State intervention in the form of social security benefits has traditionally focused on nuclear families and children: widows received benefits long before single mothers – to help them care for their children in the 'national interest'. And men could claim tax relief for supporting a daughter/housekeeper even in the 1940s. Not until 1973, when the Whitlam Labour government introduced the supporting mother's benefit, were single women granted a status of child rearer independent of men. In 1977 the benefit was extended to lone fathers (Roe 1983: 12–13).

The national preoccupation with women as dependent mothers and wives has taken many forms. One authority in 1919 even argued that all the paraphernalia of police and punishment could be scrapped 'if only mothers would understand their duty and learn how to do it' (quoted in Reiger 1982: 81). During the next decade before the 1930s depression set in, the Empire Settlement Act (1922) was passed. With associated legislation, this enabled Britain and Australia to encourage oppressed white Britons to settle in the open spaces of Australia where, together with the local population and with the help of The Racial Hygiene Movement (forerunner of the Family Planning Association), they were urged to reproduce and improve the race. At the Movement's conference in 1929 the Commonwealth Film Censor even spoke on sex and the soul. Though part of our animal nature, he argued, sex can provide an 'uplifting experience' linking man to his maker and 'the name of this stair by which men climb to god is woman' (Reiger 1982: 82). A few years later in 1938 when Australia observed the 150th anniversary of Phillip's landing, women as breeders were again celebrated in pageant and verse. An example from a poetry competition included:

> Ye girls of British race
> Famous for your beauty
> Breed fast in all your grace
> For this is your duty.
> As Anzac gave in war
> So daughters at your call
> Will quick respond the more
> To replace those that fall.
> (quoted in McQueen 1978:158)

During and after the 1930s the birth rate declined and immigration intakes dropped. The Commonwealth Arbitration Court abandoned the 'living' wage in 1931 for the principle of fixing wages according to the 'capacity of industry to pay'. Wage reductions of 10 per cent ensued in all industries and some jobs previously classified as men's work were redefined as women's work, and were consequently less well paid. The differential pay rates meant that working women provided particularly cheap labour, but unlike the introduced cheap labour from Asia and Melanesia in the last century, women could not be excluded from the country and the threat they posed to male workers continued to concern the male-dominated unions.

Those women who did stay at home and breed often faced considerable hardship and struggle, as their letters submitted as evidence in the National Health and Medical Research Council's *Inquiry into the Decline in the Birth-Rate* (1944) testify. As one woman wrote: 'The falling birth-rate is due to . . . the ancient order of master and chattel . . . Let the state pay the mother a living wage for herself and for each child and so leave her independent of her husband's pay envelope and she will have her family' (quoted in Cass 1983b: 172). The then Director General of Health, who compiled the women's written testimonies, did not question the sexual division of labour, although he noted that the social condition of the women 'must be profoundly altered if this nation is to survive' (quoted in Cass 1983b: 172).

The implementation of federal social welfare policies to promote and support fertility ensued from this Inquiry. The 1944 report denounced abortion and defined the family as the site for redistribution policies. It was assumed that women's unpaid domestic labour and childcare were the foundation of welfare, full employment and population policies. The state intervened, therefore, not to introduce increased individual wages, but to provide a 'social wage' in the form of child endowment and maternity allowances and to subsidise housing and health care (Cass 1983b: 174).

The effects of immigration on Australia's population and its costs to the state were the concern of the National Population Inquiry (NPI) in 1970. When Labour assumed power in 1972, the terms of the Inquiry were extended to consider, among other things, the abandoning of immigration control based on colour, creed and race. Australia continued to need people. In the NPI *Supplementary Report* (1978) there is a clear focus on fertility decline as a social issue, but as Cass argues, despite government's well intentioned view of the 'national interest', 'it has not been recognised that the political and economic conditions of advanced industrial capitalism have militated *against* fertility, especially the fertility of working-class women and of working-class migrant women' (1983b: 177). Like its predecessor in 1944, the 1978 *Report* assumed the traditional sexual division of labour in the family to be 'natural', and that women will leave the workforce to rear children (Cass 1983b: 181). No class analysis or feminist insight is evident in these reports. Class and gender inequalities were implicitly accepted as public expenditure in the social welfare sphere contracted. Official government compaigns to establish 'national family policies' continue to adhere to ideological notions that the family is the 'natural' unit and provider of services to the state. Cuts in the value of the social wage to women (expenditure on childcare) help sustain the dependency of women and push them into providing an 'invisible welfare system' based on their unpaid domestic labour (Cass 1983b; 185). With the depressed economic climate in the 1980s, high unemployment rates and increasing single-parent families, there has also been a transfer of female dependency from male breadwinners to the state (Roe 1983: 18). However liberating in one respect, welfare provisions have perpetuated this dependency and women remain conspicuous among the 'permanent poor'.

As the birth rate fell in the 1970s Australian women were again urged to breed. Their failure to do so was even cited as a cause for the recession, and in 1977 the Anglican Archbishop of Sydney was reported as criticising both state and federal governments for funding Women's Health and Rape Crisis Centres because they allegedly advocated easy access to abortion, promiscuity and lesbianism. According to the Archbishop, the centres 'disturb and destroy the inherited moral standards and values of our nation' and actively promote 'drastic change in normal human relationships (*SMH*, 5 October 1977). During the 1979 abortion debate in federal parliament the Minister for Health was reported as deploring the prevalence of abortion and the increased use of contraception. Both, he said, had upset planning projections and it would require a massive immigration programme to effect a population increase. Another MP concluded that Australia was on the path to self-genocide (*SMH*, 23 March 1979).

The general injunction to breed has been extended to immigrant women arriving in Australia since the Second World War, but their experiences have varied depending on their location in their culture of origin, their class position in Australia and their ability to speak English. Although women in the family occupy a central position in popular belief, in state population and welfare planning programmes, in political propaganda and in various ideologies, women do not form a homogeneous category in social life.

As government policy on family reunion prefers immediate dependants (usually the wives and daughters of men), the state exercises a stricter control over immigrant families than over local ones, ensuring that wherever possible the nuclear rather than the extended family is reproduced (Martin 1984: 117). For women from the UK, northern Europe and north America or those from middle class backgrounds with professional or managerial breadwinners from any country, or who are independent, this limitation may not prove so much of a hurdle. But women from Mediterranean and some Asian countries

> are caught squarely in the contradiction between consumption/ social reproduction and production, and are socially punished for being there. For economic reasons, for cultural reasons, from isolation and boredom, they are driven into paid work at a stage in their life cycle when they are 'supposed' to be at home caring for and rearing their families, setting up the family unit and furnishing it accordingly. (Martin 1984: 115)

For some Mediterranean and Middle Eastern women the social punishment goes further. Those from societies where women's roles are justified by strong ideologies of machismo or honour have sometimes found it difficult to sustain social relations outside their ethnic communities or even outside their families. As an Italian woman explained, after marriage 'the life of slavery then began (*vita di schiavitu*)' (Huber 1977: 23). The woman's work experience is often fraught with tension too because, although the family needs the money, the woman is not accustomed to factory work or mixing with outsiders. In some cases husbands forbid their wives to mix with Australians who are perceived to be too permissive. Where these women have been victims of sexual harassment at work they have even been afraid to tell their husbands lest they accuse them of having encouraged the advances (Bottomley 1984: 4).

Among Lebanese Muslim women, for instance, their participation rate in the workforce is even less than that for Australian women because of cultural pressures which define

> the primary role of women . . . as that of homemaker and child-bearer. This role is reinforced by various patriarchal ideologies, the most common of which is the ideology of honour. Men invest their honour in the virtue of their women and thereby idealise and control them. One consequence is that women's mobility is often very restricted since their independence is always seen as potentially threatening to the reputation of males and their families. (Humphrey 1984: 40)

Yet for those whose class position entails economic insecurity and hardship, the religious community does give support even though this in turn encourages traditional family relations and early marriage for women. For young women brought up in Australia this can lead to conflicts over gender roles, cultural identity and social continuity (Humphrey 1984: 41). Orthodox Jews have similar problems with respect to conflicts arising from Jewish law concerning religious marriage and divorce.

Among some Italian, Greek, other Mediterranean settlers, some Asians and Muslim Lebanese arranged marriages are still customary. Greeks in Australia, for example, 'are more married than Greeks in Greece' and proportionally more Greek Australian women have had their marriages arranged by parents and relatives (73 per cent) compared with women in Greece (25 per cent) (Bottomley 1984: 5,8). Arranged marriages among Punjabi Sikh farmers in Australia are also customary (de Lepervanche 1984: 154–8).

In cities where more welfare services are available, some immigrant women have rejected customary gender subordination, particularly after bashings and rapes by husbands and fathers: they have sought refuge in Women's Health Centres, Refuges and Rape Crisis Centres in the face of opposition from their men (*SMH*, 22 November 1980; Bottomley 1984: 6). These problems highlight the need for strong feminist representation from ethnic groups as the present policy of multi-culturalism, however liberating in some respects, can preserve traditions that can have unfortunate consequences for women. But some women have been on the move: in 1981 a woman of Italian immigrant origin was elected to the New South Wales Legislative Council; the Italian Federation of Workers and their Families (FILEF) has an active women's group and other groups include the Australian Arab Women's Association, the Turkish Women's Association and the Hellenic Women's Association (Bottomley 1984). Even so, ethnic politics are male-dominated and decidedly petit bourgeois in complexion; some ethnic leaders try to maintain conservative and sexist customs that have already been lost or diluted in the homeland (Bottomley 1984), and gains made for women's autonomy have been resented by these ethnic spokesmen as well as by Australian men. Multi-culturalism in Australia is still a very male ideology which does not resonate with the specificities of class and gender differences.

In any discussion of family reunion and the maintenance of communal boundaries, it is important to remember that white sexist domination has many ramifications. In the use of Depo Provera, for example, certain categories of women, including Aboriginal school-girls and some immigrant women, are more disadvantaged than others (Bottomley 1984: 4). The Australian Drug Evaluation Committee ruled in 1977 that this drug cannot be promoted as a contraceptive, but its use as a contraceptive may occur on a trial or 'investigational' basis if administered to a patient on the basis of her 'informed consent' (Fraser & Weisberg 1981). Yet Aboriginal school-girls in Oodnadatta have been given injections of Depo against their will as they have been 'living in danger' from itinerant railway workers. A local resident of the town explained that the drug had been provided by a special Aboriginal health unit within the South Australian Health Commission (*SHM*, 7 December 1984).

A curious twist to Australian racist and sexist practices has been the 'recent spectacular growth in the Filipino marriage market' (Watkins 1982: 73). Statistics from the Australian Department of Immigration show that 384 Filipino brides entered Australia in 1978–79 and 607 were introduced in 1979–80 when an additional 111 financées also migrated. More brides were expected in future years (I have heard from an unofficial estimate that there are 3000 in the country) as Australian men 'are now looking for Asian brides to fulfil what they see as the traditional role of a wife' (Watkins 1982: 82).

They describe the Asian women as 'very faithful, not forceful, and co-operative – traits they have found lacking in Australian women' (Watkins 1982: 73).

Yet the status of other Asian immigrants, mostly in working class or petit bourgeois jobs if they are not unemployed, has been recently under attack, particularly from white middle class spokesmen claiming to speak for those 'ordinary Australians' who see their jobs and way of life threatened by the 'Asianisation' of Australia. Since 1980 racist criticism of Asian settlers, especially Vietnam refugees, many of whom have entered under the family reunion provisions, has increased. Simultaneously with attacks on Aboriginal claims to land rights (particularly by mining interests), the anti-Asian racism has appeared in numerous graffiti and in the press, accompanied by calls to preserve Australia's British (or at least European) heritage. The question of who has the right to people the nation and to own its land is very definitely contested terrain, despite the state's official policy of multi-culturalism. Curiously, while some increases in Asian immigration have been met with outpourings of ethnocentrism and, it would appear, some government response, there is very little public protest about movements of foreign capital that gives rise to newspaper headlines such as 'Australia a haven for Asian investors' (*SMH*, 12 November 1984) or 'Businessmen defend the "unethical" Japanese' (*SMH*, 27 October 1984).

The most articulate critic of present immigration policy, Geoffrey Blainey, a Melbourne University professor of history, has argued that 'a family-reunion scheme is overwhelmingly a racial-reunion scheme' (1984: 98) whereas the 'typical nation practises discrimination against migrants, for the sake of national unity' (1984: 52). If Australia continued to treat all peoples of the world as equally eligible as immigrants, he writes, and the Asian percentage became the dominant stream, the 'Asian and Third World domination of the migrant lists would be self generating, and Australia would eventually become an Asian nation' (1984: 119). In the last few years, he argues, successive Australian governments have cut 'the crimson threads' of kinship with Britain and thereby disowned our past (1984: 159), and now the 'desire to turn Australia into a new nation, a nation of all nations . . . contradicts the increasing sense of national pride that has become so vivid since the Whitlam era' (1984: 153). Blainey's nationalism, like other nationalisms of the New Right, draws on the notion of a universal human nature which 'naturally' distinguishes other cultures from its own, which it prefers. By invoking 'nature' and 'natural' differences between cultural (ethnic) groups, such people can deny their racism.

CONCLUSION

In comparison with men's, women's status generally remains disadvantaged with respect to ownership of wealth, job opportunities and the sharing of power. Women have no real control over material production, the production of knowledge in general or of scientific/ technological knowledge in particular. They are poorly represented in top positions in the commercial and professional worlds, in trades unions, in universities and in parliament. When they are in paid employment they are concentrated in 'female' industries or in the lower ranks of the occupational hierarchies (Power 1975). Their average weekly wage in the 1980s has been only 67 per cent that of men's, and childcare facilities are grossly inadequate for working women (Power *et al.* 1984). Single mothers particularly feature prominently in poverty figures (Cass 1983a) and both Aboriginal and immigrant women are subject to racist as well as sexist practices. All women are currently the objects of a considerable amount of right wing rhetoric about their place in the family, even though their 'nurturing' propensities and their 'matrist' values have even been considered dangerous to the state and to civic consciousness on the grounds that they allegedly emphasise 'sensate comfort, unconditional communal support and satisfaction' all of which, according to Ronald Conway, contributed to 'Australia's steep rise in unemployment' in the 1970s (1978: 27).

Australian women have not remained passive or submissive in the face of these male constructions. Immigrant women have mobilised among themselves, Aboriginal women have been prominent in lobbying for land rights and in setting up welfare centres for their own people (Grimshaw 1981: 86). Women in general have also joined in political action in bringing about changes in the divorce and rape laws, to institute maternity leave and to introduce the anti-discrimination legislation of the 1970s and 1980s. Even so, Australian civil society and the state remain constructed in opposition to female nature, domestic life and the production of children, all of which raises the question: what kind of patriarchy are we confronting? An answer to this question can be found in the work of Carole Pateman.

As Pateman argues, one of the foundations of today's opposition

between the sexes is the modern form of partriarchy inherent in the
fraternal social contract which must be distinguished from the (European) patriarchalism of three centuries ago. Both forms accept that
'women (wives), unlike sons, were born and remained naturally subject
to men (husbands)', but the economic dependence of wives increased
with the development of capitalism and 'reinforced the appearance of a
natural subordination' (Pateman 1983: 6). Thus, although liberal
theory has argued for liberty, equality and fraternity for individuals, the
individuals have been men as 'brothers'. The social contract constitutes
then a patriarchy of men as a fraternity who exercise power over women
and who benefit from women's subordination: 'The crucial distinction
between the partriarchy of the fathers and the modern, liberal patriarchy of the brothers is that the latter is created separately from and in
opposition to the family' (Pateman 1983: 9).

This distinction informs the difference between man, constructed
as the breadwinner, protector and defender of women and woman
the breeder, a difference perhaps most vividly expressed in the state's
requirement that men in wars have had to surrender their bodies in
defence of the state in 'the truly, exemplary act of citizenship'
(Pateman 1983: 18). Not surprisingly, then, in Australia until the
1960s 'war widows headed the hierarchy of women welfare recipients'
and 'an ambivalent attitude towards women without men' prevailed
(Roe 1983: 11–12).

The 'intimate connection between masculinity, citizenship and . . .
bearing . . . arms' is opposed to the women's proper role of creating
and preserving life under male protection (Pateman 1983: 20), and
the general form of social contract is therefore 'an (apparent)
exchange of (spurious) protection for obedience. Contract gives the
appearance of voluntarism and freedom to domination and subjection that is, in many aspects, still ascriptive in character' (Pateman
1983: 21). The rights women have won as citizens have therefore only
served to 'highlight the opposition between a formal civil equality
made after a male image and the real social position of women *as
women*' (Pateman 1983: 23). As Pateman concludes:

Despite the important divisions between men of different races and
classes . . . feminists are showing how men, as men, have a
common interest; or, it is to their rational advantage to uphold the
contract, since *as men* they gain material and psychological benefits
throughout the whole of socio-political life, in the family, production and the state. (1983: 23)

Bearing Pateman's argument in mind, it is clear that, like the white race and nation of the early twentieth century, the ethnic groups and multi-cultural Australian state of today are cultural constructions created by men. Admittedly, women's traditional role has been crucial in producing and maintaining these imagined communities, yet too little is known about the specific gender, class and ethnic contexts in which women have been contributing to the 'national interest', accomplishing the state's purpose or have been excluded from it (cf. Anthias and Yuval-Davis this volume).

The rhetoric around the Bicentenary of 1988 in which multi-cultural Australia celebrated white settlement has sharpened awareness of state control of, and surveillance over, the nation, national identity and the national interest. The various ethnic groups within the state and their diverse cultures provide a focus for concern in the construction of state policies on immigration, citizenship, education and the family. Women need to be particularly vigilant in monitoring the state's version of this national interest: their own interests and the state's may well be in contradiction.

BIBLIOGRAPHY

Abbreviations:
ABS Australian Bureau of Statistics, Yearbook of Australia 1985 (Canberra, 1985)
SMH Sydney Morning Herald

Allen, J. (1979) 'Breaking into the Public Sphere', in J. Mackinolty & H. Radi (eds), *In Pursuit of Justice* (Sydney: Hale & Iremonger) 107–17.
Bacchi, C. (1980) 'Evolution, Eugenics and Women', in E. Windschuttle (ed.), *Women, Class and History* (Melbourne: Fontana/Collins) 132–56.
Baldock, C.V. (1983) 'Public Policies and the Paid Work of Women', in C.V. Baldock and B. Cass (eds), *Women, Social Welfare and the State* (Sydney: Allen & Unwin) 20–53.
Bean, C.E.W. (1981) *The Story of Anzac: The Official History of Australia in the War of 1914–18*, 2 volumes (Brisbane: University of Queensland Press).
Blainey, G. (1984) *All For Australia* (Sydney: Methuen Haynes).
Bottomley, G. (1984) 'Mediterranean Women in Australia: An Overview', paper presented at a Symposium of Mediterranean Women's Organisations, Delphi, Greece, 5–8 April.

Cass, B. (1983a) 'Redistribution to Children and to Mothers: a History of Child Endowment and Family Allowances', in C.V. Baldock & B. Cass (eds), *Women, Social Welfare and the State* (Sydney: Allen & Unwin) 54–84.

Cass, B. (1983b) 'Population Policies and Family Policies: State Construction of Domestic Life', in C.V. Baldock & B. Cass (eds), *Women, Social Welfare and the State* (Sydney: Allen & Unwin) 164–85.

Collins, J. (1984) 'Immigration and Class: the Australian Experience', in G. Bottomley and M. de Lepervanche (eds), *Ethnicity, Class and Gender in Australia* (Sydney: Allen & Unwin) 1–27.

Conway, R. (1978) *Land of the Long Weekend* (Melbourne: Sun Books).

de Lepervanche, M. (1980) 'From Race to Ethnicity', *Australian and New Zealand Journal of Sociology*, vol. 16, no. 1, 24–37.

de Lepervanche, M. *Indians in a White Australia* (Sydney: Allen & Unwin).

Evans, R., K. Saunders and K. Cronin (1975) *Exclusion, Exploitation and Extermination* (Sydney: ANZ Book Company).

Fraser, I.S., & E. Weisberg (1981) 'A Comprehensive Review of Injectable Contraception with Special Emphasis on Depo Medroxyprogesterone Acetate', *Medical Journal of Australia*, vol. 1, no. 1, special supplement.

Gammage, B. (1975) *The Broken Years: Australian Soldiers in the Great War* (Harmondsworth: Penguin).

Gordon, L. (1975) 'Race, Suicide and the Feminist Response', *Hecate: A Women's Interdisciplinary Journal*, vol. 1, no. 2, 40–53.

Grimshaw, P. (1981) 'Aboriginal Women: a Study of Culture Contact', in N. Greive & P. Grimshaw (eds), *Australian Women: Feminist Perspectives* (Melbourne: Oxford University Press) 86–94.

Horne, D. (1972) *The Australian People* (Sydney: Angus & Robertson).

Huber, R. (1977) *From Pasta to Pavlova* (Brisbane: University of Queensland Press).

Humphrey, M. (1984) 'Islamic Law in Australia', in *Islam in Australia*, Proceedings of a Seminar held at Macarthur Institute of Higher Education, Sydney, May, 36–47.

McQueen, H. (1978) *Social Sketches of Australia 1888–1975* (Harmondsworth: Penguin).

Martin, J. (1984) 'Non-English Speaking Women: Production and Social Reproduction', in G. Bottomley & M. de Lepervanche (eds), *Ethnicity, Class and Gender in Australia* (Sydney: Allen & Unwin) 109–22.

Oxley, H. (1979) 'Ockerism: the Cultural Rabbit', in P. Spearritt & D. Walker (eds), *Australian Popular Culture* (Sydney: Allen & Unwin) 190–209.

Pateman, C. (1983) 'The Fraternal Social Contract: Some Observations on Patriarchal Civil Society', paper presented to the Australian Women's Philosophy Conference, Adelaide.

Power, M. (1975) 'Women's Work is Never Done – By Men: a Socio-Economic Model of Sex-Typing in Occupations', *Journal of Industrial Relations*, vol. 17, no. 3, 225–39.

Power, M., S. Outhwaite, S. Rosewarne, J. Templeman and C. Wallace (1984) 'Writing Women Out of the Economy', paper presented to From

Margin to Mainstream: a National Conference About Women and Employment, Melbourne, 16 October.

Price, C.A. (1966) 'Post-War Migration: Demographic Background', in A. Stoller (ed.), *New Faces: Immigration and Family Life in Australia* (Melbourne: Cheshire) 11–29.

Reiger, K. (1982) 'Women's Labour Redefined: Childbearing and Rearing Advice in Australia 1880–1930s', in M. Bevedge, M. James and C. Shute (eds), *Worth Her Salt: Women at Work in Australia* (Sydney: Hale & Iremonger) 72–83.

Roe, J. (1983) 'The End is Where We Start From: Women and Welfare Since 1901', in C.V. Baldock & B. Cass (eds), *Women, Social Welfare and the State* (Sydney: Allen & Unwin) 1–19.

Saunders, K. 'Pacific Islander Women in Queensland: 1863–1907', in M. Bevedge, M. James and C. Shute (eds), *Worth Her Salt: Women at Work in Australia* (Sydney: Hale & Iremonger) 16–32.

Watkins, D. (1982) 'Filipino Brides: Slaves or Marriage Partners?' *Australian Journal of Social Issues*, vol. 17, no. 1, 73–84.

4 Mothers of the Nation: a Comparative Analysis of Nation, Race and Motherhood in Afrikaner Nationalism and the African National Congress

Deborah Gaitskell and
Elaine Unterhalter

The concept of nation has a different content according to the way in which the social forces are aligned at any particular moment and the nature of the prevailing ideologies. Far from being an incontrovertible given, 'nation' is one of the most elastic of concepts. This is particularly clear in the case in South Africa. Very different notions of nation have been developed by the dominant classes on the one hand and the dominated on the other.

Race has permeated the perceptions of nation of virtually all the dominant classes but its centrality has been most unambiguously expressed within Afrikaner nationalism. At certain points important proponents of Afrikaner nationalism have totally fused the concept of nation with that of the white race. Thus in 1972 a National Party cabinet minister, Connie Mulder, declared 'Soon there will be no black South Africans' (quoted in Lacey 1982: 3). He anticipated apartheid refined to such a point where 85 per cent of the population of his country had lost their nationality on account of their race and the South African nation had become the people identified as of white race.

Some 60 per cent of the white population of South Africa are Afrikaans-speaking. Most, but not all, Afrikaners can be deemed 'nationalists', although, as discussed below, important divisions have appeared in nationalist ranks throughout the twentieth century.

Although there has been a strand in African nationalism that has identified the nation only with the black race, this strand has never been dominant in South Africa (Lodge 1983: 80–4). The movement that has led the opposition to the political subordination of the black population, their segregation and exploitation, and which today, 75 years after its foundation, commands mass popular support is the African National Congress (ANC). The Freedom Charter, compiled in 1955 after a country-wide campaign by the ANC to collect popular views on an alternative society to that which existed under apartheid, expresses in its preamble: 'We, the people of South Africa, declare for all our country and the world to know: that South Africa belongs to all who live in it, black and white, and that no government can justly claim authority unless it is based on the will of the people' (Suttner & Cronin 1986: 262). The Freedom Charter remains the guiding manifesto of the ANC. Although the ANC is outlawed in South Africa and can only operate underground, the Freedom Charter is not banned and has been adopted in the 1980s by a number of key organisations of the mass democratic movement, most notably the student and youth congresses with more than a million members and two of the largest trade unions. While Afrikaner nationalism is dominated by a formulation of the nation that identifies special privileges for those deemed of white race, the African nationalism of the ANC is explicitly non-racial and lays great emphasis on a vision of the nation in which race is not a determinant, but democracy is.

Although there are two very different concepts of the nation ideologically and physically at war in South Africa, some observers remark there are similarities in the content of Afrikaner nationalism and African nationalism (Marks & Trapido 1987: 2, 23; Matisonn 1987: 5). This chapter looks at one such superficial similarity, the way both political organisations have constructed an ideology of 'the mother of the nation', and discusses how different the content of those ideologies are, partly because of the different concepts of the nation, partly because of the different circumstances of black and white women, and partly because the state, shaped by a complex of social forces, has itself given a different content to motherhood according to race and class. We focus particularly in each case on periods of nationalist mobilisation. This entails looking closely at Afrikaner nationalism in the post-Boer War period and the 1920s and 1930s on the one hand, and at the ANC in the 1950s, and 1970s and 1980s on the other.

MOEDERS VAN ONS VOLK: MOTHERHOOD IN AFRIKANER NATIONALISM

Throughout this century, to the extent that Afrikaner women have appeared at all in the rhetoric and imagery used for the 'ethnic mobilisation' (Adam & Giliomee 1979) of the Afrikaner *volk* ('people'), they have figured overwhelmingly as mothers.

Three different representations of Afrikaner motherhood since the turn of the century can be identified and each relates to a changing conception of race and nation. Despite some overlapping, a rough periodisation is possible, corresponding to the periods after the three watershed dates in 1902 (the Afrikaner defeat by the British in the South African War, entailing imperial rule over their formerly independent Boer republics); 1914 (the formation of the first Afrikaner National Party – NP); and 1948 (the accession to power of the first wholly Afrikaner nationalist government, which has remained the ruling party ever since). In each case, the nation is perceived differently. First, the Afrinaker nation mourns as a suffering victim; then on the basis of racial and cultural distinctiveness, the nation mobilises to redress political and economic disadvantage; finally, the Afrikaner nation attains state power completely independently but is eventually compelled because of challenges to its authority to expand its appeal to all members of the white race and then attempt to enlarge the boundaries of the nation to encompass black groups. Notions of motherhood shift accordingly.

In the first phase, after 1902, Afrikaner motherhood is exalted as saintly in suffering, admired for stoicism in victimisation, its strength an inspiration to the rest of the defeated nation. The emphasis is on nobility, passivity, virtuous nurturing and protection of children. This appears to be an image shaped by male cultural entrepreneurs, the women themselves as silent as in their stereotypical portrayal. In the aftermath of the Boer War, the former Boer generals, Botha and Smuts, were working to build conciliation between English- and Afrikaans-speaking white South Africans – and were duly rewarded with the leadership of the first government of a united South Africa, in 1910. The less prosperous, more politically threatened segment in the Afrikaner community – petit bourgeois journalists, teachers, clerics and writers – however, began building a more exclusive nationalist movement in which their occupational group could be assured of a stake (Hofmeyr 1987). The Second Language Movement of those years produced Afrikaans literature which twinned the recent cycle of suffering and death in the war with the earlier suffering of the *Voortrekkers* (Afrikaner emigrants from the British Cape Colony in the 1830s), not only at the hands of the British but especially from the Zulu and other African peoples encountered in that 'Great Trek'. The sufferings of Afrikaner mothers were central to the emotive portrayal of the nation's agony since both were seen as blameless victims. Thus in Gustav Preller's historical writings about the Trek, 'the noble blood of women, girls and tiny babes' matted the grass after a Zulu attack, 'women's breasts were severed, their bodies mutilated and ravished', nursing infants pierced with Zulu spears (Preller, quoted Moodie 1975: 6). Likewise, in the early accounts of Boer suffering during the war, the 26 000 women and children who died in the British concentration camps loom large, the outrage and pathos of their fate a staple of the nationalist litany on into the 1950s (le Roux 1986: 196). Those days in the camps were 'days of lamentation and bitterness . . . The moaning and weeping of sick mothers, the crying and pleading of little children dying of hunger in cold tents mounted up to heaven. But in vain' (Smith, quoted Moodie 1975: 9–10).

One of the few poems of lament of this time to give great prominence to Afrikaner women, C.L. Leipoldt's *Vrede-Aand* ('Peace Night'), has a powerful evocation of this maternal loss and tribulation. But it also pays tribute to the women as 'the strongest of us all' for, helped by God, the 'heroine and wife' bore 'the heaviest burden'. The inspiration of women's spirituality is stressed, for women's soul is the 'leading light'. As a final apostrophe, he exclaims, 'Woman! Our nation's treasure' (Grove & Harvey 1962). Again, it was the agony of the camps, woman as suffering mother of the nation, which the Women's Monument, opened at Bloemfontein in 1913, commemorated. Within a circular enclosure stands a bare-headed woman, holding a dying child, another woman in Voortrek-ker dress staring out across the veld. In panels on either side, again mothers and children feature, first entering the concentration camp (under the caption 'For freedom, volk and fatherland') and then an emaciated child dying in a camp tent, his mother by his side, a panel headed 'If you do not despair, I shall not forsake you' (Moodie 1975: 19). Maternal desolation and isolation were to embody the deep sense of devastation which the people felt in defeat.

In the second phase of Afrikaner nationalism, motherhood within the volk is perceived as far more active and mobilising. This coincides with the attempt of the disinherited Afrikaners to rebuild their cultural distinctiveness for parity with or even domination of the English. The home is focused on as women's appropriate arena for fostering Afrikaner national identity through their child-rearing and domestic responsibilities. These were the years after the two former Boer republics and the two British colonies had come together in the Union of South Africa, ruled by coalition Afrikaner–English governments which consciously strove from 1910–24 and again from 1933–48 to minimise division between the two white 'races' (to use the terminology of the time). Only from 1924–33, and even then in coalition with white Labour Party politicians for the first five years of that 'Pact', did the more vehement Afrikaner nationalists hold power. But it was in those years that Afrikaans (instead of Dutch) achieved equal official status with English (in 1925). Hertzog had perceived the Afrikaner nation as needing to mobilise to overcome its inequality *vis-à-vis* the English; for the second wave of nationalism beginning later in this period, parity was not enough and Afrikanerdom had further economic and cultural nationalist mobilising to do.

Popular literature like the magazine *Brandwag*, launched in 1910, aimed very specifically to capture the home for the Afrikaner language, culture and people. It chose to concentrate 'on a point where the land lies unprotected', for it was 'determined to steal a place in the Afrikaans family which is at present empty or is filled with foreign nonsense like Home Notes, Home Chat and Home Journal' (quoted in Hofmeyr 1987: 114). There was, Isabel Hofmeyr suggests, a community of interest between the Afrikaner women seeking to enhance their importance and status within both the domestic sphere and the limited public arena open to them in the women's welfare and political movements starting up after the Boer War, and the men of the Afrikaner Language Movement. For the male writers and ideologies there was 'an over-riding interest in making the Afrikaans family a solid reality' because the home was at that stage almost the only place where some form of Afrikaans was consistently spoken. Anglicisation was proceeding apace in the workplace, for the urban economy was at this stage largely in the hands of English-speaking capitalist concerns and the Labour Party espousing the white workers' cause had English roots. In church until 1918–19 ordinary Afrikaners heard Dutch sermons and sang Dutch hymns, while it was hard for parents to ignore the lure of English education when language could prove a vital asset for employment. It was 'not for nothing that Afrikaans was so frequently called "the mother tongue"'; if anyone was going to socialise children as Afrikaners in this situation where the male-dominated worlds of church and work used Dutch or English, it was the women, hence it was essential for Afrikaners to capture the home for the new nationalist outlook (Hofmeyr 1987: 113).

From the mid-1920s it was *Huisgenoot* ('Family/Home Companion') which, with its less literary and more pictorial appeal, became perhaps the most widely read magazine in South Africa. Through articles, advertisements, pictures and stories, such journals were engaged in redefining and repackaging Afrikaner everyday life to portray what was 'authentically' Afrikaans in 'Food, architecture, interior decoration, dress, etiquette, health, humour, landscape, monuments, the plastic arts, music . . . and so on'. Thus a woman who adopted this all-embracing ethnic identity and nationalist loyalty could increase her status at home, but also within women's organisations, 'by appearing publicly as an Afrikaner woman, who also taught others how to be Afrikaner women' (Hofmeyr 1987: 114). This was a devotion to be poured out not just towards families but also the volk. By contrast, in the nationalist appeals of African community, the home could not feature as a starting point of strength in quite the same way. The shattering effect of conquest and apartheid on the African family meant the school, the workplace and the community replaced the importance of the home as a centre of nationalist mobilisation. Afrikaners in the 1920s and 1930s, however, hoped their homes would be a maternal powerhouse of domestic ethnic mobilisation.

There was much more ambivalence in the Afrikaner community about women's contribution in the public political arena as opposed to the domestic sphere, precisely because of woman's supposedly divinely ordained role as wife and mother. By the 1920s the Women's Enfranchisement Association of the Union (WEAU) had been campaigning for a decade for the female franchise but its small, exclusively white membership was almost entirely English-speaking, educated, privileged urban women (Walker 1982: 21). Afrikaner women's hostility to the suffrage movement because of its image of 'foreignness' and imperialist sympathies was bolstered by, for instance, the opposition of the Dutch Reformed Church (DRC – to which the vast majority of Afrikaners belong) to women's suffrage. A 1920 DRC synod condemned it on biblical grounds: the vote belonged 'to the man as the head of the family' – three biblical texts were quoted at this point – 'and not to the women who, in accordance with the story of creation, was given to man as a helpmate (Genesis 2.18)' (Walker 1979: 22). So women's auxiliary role in the family precluded the vote.

And yet, no doubt in their 'helpmate' role, the Women's National Party was founded in July 1915 to work in conjunction with Hertzog's party. It was the growing support for female suffrage from these Afrikaner nationalist women as the 1920s progressed, and in the context of increased Afrikaner urbanisation and female employment, that led the NP to re-evaluate its stance. Race intertwined with nation and gender in a complex way because of South Africa's constitutional specificities: the nationalist premier Hertzog espoused votes for white women because that would dilute the black vote in the Cape. (In the African and 'coloured' franchise there was a legacy of its nineteenth-century status as a British colony.)

Thus in 1930, under Hertzog, white women were enfranchised in a racially exclusive Bill: 'In this Act . . . "woman" means a woman who is wholly of European parentage, extraction or descent' (Walker 1979: 23–4). It could be argued, then, that the female 'political nation' in South Africa was constituted in racially exclusive terms by state policy for the country as a whole some years before this was the case for men. (Cape Africans lost the vote for the Union parliament in 1936 and Cape Coloureds in 1956.) But in a sense this was only possible for white women precisely because of the nature and basis of their political mobilisation – around an exclusive ideology of motherhood and the isolation within the home which it implied.

In a sense, the major political watershed of 1948 does not really herald the third phase of Afrikaner nationalist conceptions of motherhood and the state. The creation and defence of the Afrikaner home continued to be the Afrikaner woman's prime service to the volk into the 1960s. Only in that decade was there a marked shift to a more inclusive conception of the white nation, which in turn, particularly by the late 1970s, led to a broader appeal to black and white mothers which has become in the 1980s an attempt to usurp the fully national call to women of the ANC.

The changing conception of the white nation was rooted in the fact that an Afrikaner capitalist class came into being. Afrikaners in the cities had made remarkable progress in their attempts to catch up with the long-entrenched wealth of the urban English speaker. The home was therefore no longer in the forefront of ethnic struggle.

Instead of being a key base from which to reconstruct the Afrikaner nation, it became a focus for the display of the new-found prosperity which ethnic mobilisation had made possible. Afrikaner wives and mothers moved into a less defensive phase, proud of the affluent lifestyle which they now shared, many of them, with their fellow whites. Instead of anglicisation absorbing Afrikanerdom, both language groups had a materialistic consumer culture in common.

Afrikaner women occupied a less important role in nation building in these years. In a notorious incident, they were urged to 'have a baby for Republic Day', to celebrate five years since leaving the Commonwealth (1961–6), but their ideological and political contribution as opposed to their biologically reproductive role was much marginalised. Their invisibility in the public political arena persisted.

The broadening of nationalist support among the white population at large from the mid-1960s (Stultz 1974: 165) was attended by a new sharp division within Afrikanerdom from the late 1960s, the first serious fracturing of their ethnic unity in two decades and a split which intensified further in the early 1980s. Much of this bitter in-fighting has implicitly been about the blurring of the boundaries of the nation: first to accommodate English speakers within the wider white nation and now latterly even appearing to expand the white nation to accommodate or effect the alignment of the other two minority races, the coloureds and Indians. Thus, just as Hertzog split with Botha and Smuts in 1914 over relations with Britain and English-speaking whites, and Malan did in turn with Hertzog in 1934, so the HNP ('Re-established' Nationalist Party) in 1969 and the Conservative Party in 1982 have broken nationalist ranks.

Afrikaner mothers have been mobilised in this in-fighting in at least two ways: firstly to help defend the nation against 'total onslaught' portrayed as coming both from beyond its borders and from within the local black population; and secondly to try to establish contact with co-optable members of other racial groups. The image of motherhood is therefore contradictory. It is both that of the mother–defender of the nation and that of the mother identifying with other mothers in the nation to help preserve a disappearing status quo.

The mobilisation of Nationalist Party women was being pursued in the late 1970s within the militaristic framework which was becoming pervasive in South Africa society. An NP pamphlet of 1978, *Women our Silent Soldiers*, compiled by wives of cabinet ministers and edited by the party's Chief Information Officer, called for party loyalty and solidarity within 'the total onslaught on us as a nation' (Goodwin

1984: 222 ff. for pamphlet quotes). Official propaganda was anxious to assure Afrikaner women that they were just as important as 'the boys on the border': 'women are the indispensable "soldiers" within our country's borders and their spiritual power is South Africa's secret weapon'. Women were also 'doing service' every day, 'without call-up instructions, without military pay, but in the service of the things which are dear to us – our families, our countries, our nation'.

Ostensibly the focus for Afrikaner women's nationalist activity has not changed from the pre-1948 period: it was still within the home that their service to country and nation were primarily to be performed. But the home's insertion into a wider context in which whites are warding off threats to their survival is emphasised throughout. Women are not now being urged to make Afrikaner homes but to defend them from hostile forces and, by their competent coping with family finances, for instance, help free the male members of their households to play their part in the inevitable military struggle. But the maternal education of the soldier is vital: as the 1978 pamphlet emphasises 'A woman's most important task is the educational task. A child develops pride in his cultural assets, his language, his nation and his country largely through his mother's guidance.'

In this third phase of heightened popular mobilisation against apartheid and increased international pressure on the South African state Afrikaner women are also lending themselves to inter-racial ventures with an emphasis on the common experience of motherhood across race divides, apparently attempting to pre-empt the ANC's efforts in this direction. Frede van Rooyen founded Kontak in 1976 after the Soweto revolt had begun. By 1983, appointed by the Minister of Internal Affairs, she chaired a committee trying to bring coloured and other groups closer, her warm personality and enthusiasm an asset to the state in the run-up to the launch of the new constitution. When the boundaries of the political nation were about to be extended, Afrikaner women were enlisted to promote reconciliation.

The further extension of this strategy comes in the national 'bridge-building' campaign started in October 1986, led by NP woman MP, Rina Venter, and consciously evoking common motherhood which Afrikaner women share with black: 'They are starting discussion groups and social groups and are inviting them to tea, where they discuss their problems . . . They want to understand how they feel about their political aspiration, their children's situation – things like that' (*Star*, 3 October 1986). A social worker and former president of the South African *Vrouefederasie* ('Women's Federation'), Dr Venter saw her foremost role as a mother. Her work, however, 'has left her aware of women's strength in unity, and she believes in their ability to triumph over violence, self-interest and political wrangling to join in their common interests as mothers and creators of life' (*Star*, 1 November 1986). The version of motherhood here is crucial: mothers are still seen in a very limited domestic role, united in a concern for their children. Unlike the ANC case, a focus on motherhood does not open up broader issues of women's situation and need for emancipation. Furthermore, when the situation of mothers in different race groups is in fact so manifestly different, and in a context where radical transformation of South African society is not on the agenda, 'bridge building' on the basis that the home is what mothers have in common becomes farcical.

Thus the notion of Afrikaner motherhood, its relation to the state and its contribution to national struggles, has gone through major shifts over time, as Afrikaner power in South Africa has suffered serious setbacks, then gradually reasserted itself, then faced new crises of legitimation. In the first phase, the nation's defeat in the Boer War was most feelingly focused on and remembered in the fact of the suffering of Afrikaner mothers. In the second phase, the national call for mobilisation of political support for separate Afrikaner identity as well as the mobilisation of Afrikaner wealth had its counterpart in domestic cultural mobilisation which was seen as pre-eminently the work of women as mothers. In the third phase, after some years when Afrikaner mothers rejoiced in being able to display the successful achievement of financially secure and culturally distinct homes, the power of motherhood has been invoked to assist in the survival of white domination. From the point of view of the regime mothers have a crucial role in personally supporting and validating military solutions to the opposition to apartheid, on the one hand, while on the other the cultural distinctiveness of their maternal role is now being downplayed in favour of the potential support of the white government which it may be possible to augment via inter-racial contact among mothers based on their common biological role. These changing conceptions of motherhood have clearly had their roots in material reality, in the social and economic circumstances of Afrikaner women. The suffering mothers and children of the early iconography reflected not only the grim reality of the 26 000 deaths in British concentration camps, but also the hardships of re-establishing family life after the war. Physically, motherhood for whites involved suffering, not least because white infant mortality rates in the first decades of the twentieth century were high by the standards of the day. The links are particularly striking in the second phase, at the height of concern about the problem of newly urbanised Afrikaner-speaking 'poor whites' struggling to survive in town.

The sharp contrast between the white working class suburbs of Johannesburg and the more affluent parts of the city, for instance, in respect of infant mortality rates intensified in the depression years of 1929–30 (Unterhalter 1982: 631). Social investigators also set much store by the contribution mothers could make to combating poverty and racial 'degeneracy' and this provides further explanation for the emphasis of popular Afrikaner literature of the interwar period on woman's home-making role.

In the third phase of Afrikaner motherhood, solidarity with English-speaking mothers was indeed rooted in the major shift in economic fortunes which had occurred by the 1970s. In 1978, 60 per cent of the white labour force in public and semi-public jobs were Afrikaans, while the Afrikaner share of the private sector had grown from 9.6 per cent in 1938–9 to 20.8 per cent in 1975. Income distribution between the two white groups had also evened up: in 1946, whites earned 74 per cent of the income in South Africa, the English getting 44.5 and the Afrikaners 29.5 per cent; by 1976, each got exactly half (31.5 per cent) of the whites' 63 per cent share of national income (Adam & Giliomee 1979: 165, 172).

MOTHERS OF THE NATION: MOTHERHOOD AND THE AFRICAN NATIONAL CONGRESS

In posters, pamphlets, songs and speeches in the postwar period, and particularly in the phases of mass popular mobilisation in the 1950s and again in the 1970s and 1980s the ANC, and the mass democratic organisations that share its aspirations, have laid much stress on the image of the mother; indeed the general appeal to all women has been in terms of their common potential experience of motherhood, although there have been important qualitative differences in the portrayal of the mother in different periods.

In the 1950s the major anti-apartheid women's organisation in South Africa was the Federation of South African Women (FSAW), whose largest affiliate was the ANC Women's League. The FSAW campaigned vigorously against the introduction of passes for African women, which would regulate where African women could live and work. In their campaign they stressed the identity of African women as mothers. For example, a statement presented by the FSAW to local government officials throughout the country in 1957 stressed: 'As wives and mothers we condemn the pass laws and all they imply' (quoted in Kimble & Unterhalter 1983: 26). Frances Baard, a trade union organiser and member of the ANC Women's League and FSAW in the 1950s recalled the discussions among women in the anti-pass campaign:

> We knew that you would be carrying a child, or have your child on your back, and the police will be coming behind you wanting your pass and you won't be able to run away and jump over that fence there and that will be the time the police will get you, or else your child will fall and get hurt because you are trying to run away from the police. And then who is going to look after the children when they take you to jail because you haven't got your pass, or your pass is not right? We explained to the women what would happen if we accepted these passes and no one wanted them. (Baard 1986: 47–8)

Motherhood is stressed partly because this is seen as a common experience of women, in towns and rural areas, in wage employment or working in the informal sector. It also seems that the outrage at the introduction of passes for women focuses on women's status as mothers. The implicit reasoning runs that as mothers African women deserve better treatment than the brutality routinely handed out to their men.

In its campaign to win the support of white women for African women's opposition to passes, the FSAW also stressed motherhood, but here the importance of this appears to be because motherhood was an experience black and white women shared. A pamphlet distributed by the FSAW in 1958 in white residential areas appealed to white women on the issue of passes for African women: 'In the name of humanity, can you as a woman, as a mother, tolerate this?' (quoted in Kimble & Unterhalter 1983: 26). The 1960s was a decade of severe repression in South Africa; the ANC was forced underground, and mass democratic organisations ceased to function. However, in the 1970s, initially locally and then regionally, organised opposition re-emerged as black workers went on strikes and began to build up trade unions and school and university students initiated

protests at their inferior education which escalated, in the face of
vicious police shootings of unarmed children in Soweto in 1976, into a
year-long uprising in which official buildings were burned, local
communities galvanised into rejection of the regime and thousands of
young people left the country to join the ANC and its armed struggle
against the apartheid regime.

In the anger and the commitment to national liberation that were
generated in this period there is frequent reference to the totemic
symbol of the mother. In a collection of poems by ANC women
published in 1983 there is a section on the Soweto events and their
aftermath. Out of eight poems in this section five are about
motherhood. There are two distinct images of mothers: first, there is
that of the suffering careworn mother, whose pain goads her daughter to join the liberation struggle. For example Rebecca Matlou, in
her poem entitled 'Mother Patriot' describes a woman shot dead in
the streets of Soweto in June 1976, and ends 'She must be avenged.'
The second image is of the mother, in her suffering, nurturing the
revolution. In Baleka Kgositsile's poem the mother inspires the
children with commitment to revolution:

> your sweat and tears
> let our future burn in them
> that they create
> years of the child
> let their hunger
> bear their anger
> let our children live
> and live
> (Matlou 1983: 44)

In a similar vein Ilva Mackay in her poem 'Mayibuye' fuses the image
of the mother with the revolution, so that on liberation 'our mothers
shall be returned to us' (Mackay 1983a: 46).

Young people were prominent in the uprising of 1976, which partly
might account for the stress on images of motherhood; there was also
a sense, in this period, that after the long period in which resistance
had lain dormant, repressed, it was now being reborn, and this sense
too might have inspired so many poems around the theme of
motherhood. The images of motherhood suggest strength and suffering and sadness. The mother is an inspiration to the daughter, but it is
the daughter who is the protector of the mother and in that guise and

in her decision to join the struggle and build a new society becomes the mother to future unborn generations. This appears an interesting contrast with Afrikaner nationalist literature, where it is the self-sacrificing mother, whose sacrifice rather than whose strength is the inspiration, generally to the *son* who is the poet.

From the late 1970s to the present the actions of the armed wing of the ANC Umkhontho we Sizwe, operating underground in South Africa, began to increase in number and mass democratic organisations were recreated. Many women's organisations were established and began to build regional and national structure and campaign on many issues. As in the 1950s there is once again an appeal to women of all races in terms of their common motherhood. So Albertina Sisulu, president of the United Democratic Front (UDF), the umbrella body representing some 400 local and regional anti-apartheid organisations, in an address to one thousand people at the University of Cape Town in June 1986 said: 'No selfrespecting woman can stand aside and say she is not involved while police are hunting other mothers' children like wild dogs in the townships . . . A mother is a mother, black or white. Stand up and be counted with other women' (*Argus*, 3 June 1986). The National Executive Committee of the ANC, in its address to the South African people in January 1987 issued this call:

> Black mothers have to live with the agony of having to bury their children every day. Too often they have to search for their sons and daughters who have perhaps been arrested or perhaps disappeared forever without trace. Across the barricades, the white mothers see their children transformed and perverted into mindless killers who will not stop at murdering the unarmed, and will surely turn their guns on the very mothers who today surrender their sons willingly or unwillingly to the South African death force. These black and white mothers must reach across the divide created by the common enemy of our people and form a human chain to stop, now and forever, the murderous rampage of the apartheid system. (African National Congress 1987: 8)

The same speech also affirmed:

> The mothers of the nation, the womenfolk as a whole are the titans of our struggle . . . Our revolutionary movement has long recognised the fact that an oppressive social order such as ours could not but enslave women in a particularly brutal way. One of the greatest

prizes of the democratic movement must therefore be the unshack-
ling of the women. (African National Congress 1987: 8)

In all these calls there is a fusion of women and mothers. This must
partly be read in the context of the vernacular African languages
where the word for adult woman and the word for mother are the
same and in the context of African societies, where the upbringing
of children is much more widely shared between households than is
the case in white areas. But these calls are also predicated on an
appeal to qualities of motherhood, like care and concern, which
straddle racial boundaries and which are seen to be powerful forces
that can be harnessed to destroy apartheid and create national
unity. In contrast to the appeal to women as mothers in the 1950s,
the first period of mass mobilisation, the focus now is not so much
on outrage at the treatment of mothers, but at the power mothers
exercise in society, which itself places on the agenda questions of
women's emancipation.

In many ways the changing perception of motherhood, particularly the contrast between the first phase and the third, arises out of
the changing circumstances of women. In the 1950s still a relatively
small percentage of women were wage earners: only 23 per cent of
women of all races aged 15–59 in 1950, compared with 33 per cent in
1980 (Jaffee & Caine 1986: 11). A sizeable number of women who
were mothers, both black and white, were dependent on the wages
of male workers. Within the cities where the ANC drew its major
support many of the women members worked in the informal sector
and lived in households with a number of male relatives (Kimble &
Unterhalter 1983: 22–9). In these circumstances it is hardly surprising that motherhood was perceived as a status that needed protection. In the 1980s, as well as a very marked increase in the number
of women employed in wage labour, there is also a significant
increase in the number of female-headed households. A study based
on the 1980 census found that 30 per cent of African households in
metropolitan areas, 47 per cent of households in bantustan towns
and 59 per cent of households in bantustan rural areas were headed
by women (Simkins 1986: 33–8).

There appears a marked correlation between women's political
activism and women bringing up families on their own (Cole 1986:
Unterhalter 1988). These material circumstances of black women –
their increasing wage employment, their increasing hardship
because of living without the support of male relatives and their

increasing mobilisation into women's organisations, trade unions, street committees and civic associations – seem to go a considerable way to explaining the new vision of motherhood in the ANC as something dynamic and activist, rather than passively in need of protection. In the 1980s it appears that it is largely highly educated, upper middle class, white women who have identified with black women, partly as an extension of their professional work as lawyers, teachers or social workers. The image of motherhood expressed in the speeches might well touch that embodied in their work. By contrast, in the 1950s the white women activists were mainly working in the progressive organisations as secretaries or journalists, often part-time, as they had young children, and thus probably shared protective ideas of motherhood.

Political pressures from within the dominant classes: combined in the first phase to force the regime to legislate for a particular form of nation and particular conditions of motherhood for the black population. The nation was conceived as segregated on racial lines and the state was prepared to suppress political organisations like the ANC and the black trade union movement in order to achieve this. It was against this background that the politics of protecting the non-racial democratic nation was created. Within its concept of the nation the regime dictated under what circumstances a black woman could be a mother, where she had to live and work, who she could marry and have sexual relations with.

In the second phase the regime, still supported by the same social forces from within the dominant classes, sought not only to segregate the nation according to race, but to create separate nations for Africans according to ethnic classifications and to decree South Africa as a nation of only those deemed white. Even more stringent controls were placed on where black women might live with their children, as African women with children were perceived by the regime as a threat to the strategy of returning all Africans to the bantustans. Act 42 of 1964 removed the right of African women to settle in urban areas, even though their fathers and husbands might be legally resident and working in those areas. From 1967 it became impossible for women from the bantustans even to take work legally in the urban areas as they were not allowed to register with the labour bureaus from which the contract workers were chosen. In the view of the ruling National Party, as expressed by a member of parliament for a white middle class area: 'We do not want the Bantu woman here simply as an adjunct to the procreative capacity of the Bantu population' (quoted in Simons 1968: 282). The severe hardships these policies imposed on African women, condemned to poverty in the bantustans and constantly harassed in pass raids, incensed the children of 1976, who joined the uprising (Strachan 1984). Within schools, universities and churches, relatively untouched by the repression of the political organisations the ideology of the suffering black nation rising against its oppressor was created, strongly influenced initially by notions of black consciousness but politically oriented to the aspirations of the ANC for a non-racial democratic state (Lodge 1983: 321–62). The actual experience of the suffering of mothers shaped the articulation of the ideology of motherhood and influenced the notion of nation in this period.

In the third phase cracks began to appear amidst the social forces supporting the regime. Important sectors of monopoly capitalism and some members of the white petit bourgeoisie began to mount a critique of the regime, largely because of its failure to secure lasting economic growth or political stability. Some representatives of these classes saw a non-racial democratic state as the only form of state able to secure the conditions for the reproduction of capitalist accumulation. Sectors of the white working class and petit bourgeoisie, at the other end of the political spectrum, opposed the regime because of its limited exercise in constitutional change, giving segregated parliamentary representation to coloureds and Indians, allowing the formation of black trade unions and reformulating the pass laws. These disputes in the ruling bloc partly arise from the growing mobilisation of the population and their success in articulating their grievances and insisting the ANC must be unbanned and the democratic rights of all South Africans must be recognised; equally the divisions within the ruling bloc provide a wedge which allows the mass democratic movement and the ANC to try to detach important allies from the regime. Within this context the regime has developed an ideology of the nation facing a 'total onslaught'. The nation is no longer identified only with those deemed white, but is expanded to encompass all those, white and black, who oppose the national liberation movement. In its search for black allies the regime has made important concessions with regard to conditions of motherhood. The pass laws were formally abolished in 1986, although important restrictions remain on the movement of African women – many thousands have flocked into urban areas outside the bantustans; the citizenship rights of certain Africans, who were deemed aliens as citizens of bantustans that had been decreed independent, were restored; the legislation outlawing inter-racial marriages was repealed. While these concessions in no way amount to support for black mothers they were conceived as an attempt to divide the African population. In the event, the reforms have proved too little too late and have only further spurred the organisations and militancy of black women, transforming their perception of motherhood from a protective status to a dynamic force for change.

CONCLUSION

Superficially, one can trace similarities in the way both Afrikaner and African nationalists have viewed and used motherhood in their periods of mobilisation for power. The suffering Boer War mothers are exalted and provide a stimulus to national mobilisation just as the suffering pass-carrying mothers or the mothers of Soweto did. But a different concept of the nation operates, an exclusive Afrikaner nation as opposed to the ANC belief in the non-racial democratic South African nation. Furthermore, the suffering of motherhood has led in the ANC to a call for women's emancipation; this has never been part of the trajectory of Afrikaner nationalism, where women have consciously been kept in the home and out of public life.

Other important contrasts exist also. When the power of the state was imposing passes, African women saw the need for allies and addressed a cross-racial appeal to other mothers. For Afrikaner women, their current resort to cross-racial appeals comes when their tenure of state power is perceived to be threatened by the growth of the opposition movement. Their response early in the century to the threat of anglicisation was not to seek allies but, with ethnic logic, to build up group strength partly through an exclusive, distinctive Afrikaner motherhood. Political rights for women became a priority only when their use to race and nation was clear, and they have not displaced the centrality of women in the home from Afrikaner ideology.

We began by describing the nation as the most elastic of concepts. Motherhood, this discussion of Afrikaner and African nationalist views has made clear, is likewise a very fluid and manipulable notion, especially in the context of a divided society where class and race divisions overlap. There have been very strong parallels between the form in which the nation is perceived and the form in which motherhood is viewed. Appeals to motherhood have been couched in ethnically very exclusive terms as well as in racially inclusive ways. The different circumstances of black and white mothers have shaped the relation between ideas of nation, state and motherhood. Legislation has made motherhood materially much easier and potentially more fulfilling for some groups than others, highlighting the contradiction between white assertions of the nobility of mothers and their destructions and denigration of motherhood and family life for black people. In the present, motherhood is explicitly part of the terminology and strategy of struggle of both Afrikaner nationalism and the ANC, but the implications of motherhood remain very different on both sides, just as both sides envisage a very different future for women and the nation as a whole.

BIBLIOGRAPHY

Adam, H. & H. Giliomee (1979) *Ethnic Power Mobilized: Can South Africa Change?* (New York and London: Yale University Press).

African National Congress (1987) *8 January 1987 ANC Calls for Advance to People's Power* (Lusaka/London: ANC).

Baard, F. (1986) *My Spirit is not Banned* (Harare: Zimbabwe Publishing House).

Brink, E. (1987) '"Maar 'n Klomp 'Factory' Meide": Afrikaner Family and Community on the Witwatersrands during the 1920s', in B. Bozzoli (ed.), *Class, Community and Conflict: South African Perspectives* (Johannesburg: Raven Press).

Carter, G. (1958) *The Politics of Inequality: South Africa since 1948* (New York: Prager).

Cole, J. (1986) 'When Your Life is Bitter You do Something: Women and Squatting in the Western Cape Tracing the Origins of Crossroads and the Role of Women in its Struggle', in D. Kaplan (ed.), *South African Research Papers* (Department of Economic History, University of Cape Town).

de Klerk, W.A. (1976) *The Puritans in Africa: a Story of Afrikanerdom* (Harmondsworth: Penguin Books; first published 1975).

Goodwin, J. (1984) *Cry Amandla! South African Women and the Question of Power* (New York and London: Africana Publishing Company).

Grove, A.P. & C.J.D. Harvey (1962) *Afrikaans Poems with English Translations* (Cape Town: Oxford University Press).

Hofmeyr, I. (1987) 'Building a Nation from Words: Afrikaans Language, Literature and Ethnic Identity, 1902–1924', in S. Marks & S. Trapido (eds), *The Politics of Race, Class and Nationalism in Twentieth Century South Africa* (Harlow: Longman).

Jaff, F. (1975) *Women South Africa Remembers* (Cape Town: Howard Timmins).

Jaffee, G. and C. Caine (1986) 'The Incorporation of African Women into the Industrial Workforce: its Implications for the Women's Question in South Africa', unpublished paper presented at the conference on The South African Economy after Apartheid, Centre for African Studies, University of York.

Kimble, J. and E. Unterhalter (1983) '"We Opened the Road for You, You Must Go Forward". ANC Women's Struggles, 1912–1982', *Feminist Review*, vol. 12, 11–36.

Lacey, M. (1982) 'Resettlement Policy in its Historical Context', in E. Walt (ed.), *South Africa: a Land Divided* (Johannesburg: Black Sash).

le Roux, P. (1986) 'Growing up an Afrikaner', in S. Burman & P. Reynolds (eds), *Growing up in a Divided Society: The Contexts of Childhood in South Africa* (Johannesburg: Raven Press).

Lodge, T. (1983) *Black Politics in South Africa since 1945* (London: Longman).

Mackay, I. (1983) 'Mayibuye', in S. Molefe (ed.), *Malibongwe. ANC Women: Poetry is also their Weapon* (Stockholm: African National Congress).

Marks, S. & S. Trapido (1987) 'The Politics of Race, Class and Nationalism', in S. Marks & S. Trapido (eds), *The Politics of Race, Class and Nationalism in Twentieth Century South Africa* (London: Longman).

Matisonn, J. (1987) 'Meeting the ANC in West Africa: from Dakar to Burkina Faso', *Work in Progress*, vol. 49, 3–5.

Matlou, R. (1983) 'Mother Patriot', in S. Molefe (ed.), *Malibongwe. ANC Women: Poetry is also their Weapon* (Stockholm: African National Congress).

Moodie, T.D. (1975) *The Rise of Afrikanerdom: Power, Apartheid and Afrikaner Civil Religion* (Berkeley and London: University of California Press).

O'Meara, D. (1983) *Volkskapitalisme: Class, Capital and Ideology in the Development of Afrikaner Nationalism, 1934–48* (Cambridge: Cambridge University Press).

Simkins, C. (1986) 'Household Composition and Structure in South Africa', in S. Burman & P. Reynolds (eds), *Growing up in a Divided Society: The Contexts of Childhood in South Africa* (Johannesburg: Raven Press).

Simons, H.J. (1968) *African Women: their Legal Status in South Africa* (London: C. Hurst).

Strachan, B. (1983) *Never on our Knees: Youth in Apartheid South Africa* (London: United Nations Association of Youth).

Suttner, R. & J. Cronin (1986) *Thirty Years of the Freedom Charter* (Johannesburg: Raven Press).

Stultz, N.M. (1974) *Afrikaner Politics in South Africa, 1934–1948* (Berkeley and Los Angeles: University of California Press).

Unterhalter, B. (1982) 'Inequalities in Health and Disease: the Case of Mortality Rates for the City of Johannesburg, South Africa, 1910–1979', *International Journal of Health Services*, vol. 12, no. 4, 154–71.

Unterhalter, E. (1988) 'Class, Race and Gender: the Social and Economic Origins of Women's Resistance to Apartheid', in J. Lonsdale (ed.), *South Africa in Question* (London: James Currey).

Walker, C. (1979) *The Women's Suffrage Movement in South Africa* (Cape Town: Centre for African Studies, UCT).

Walker, C. (1982) *Women and Resistance in South Africa* (London: Onyx Press).

Newspapers

Argus, Cape Town
Star, Johannesburg

5 Sexuality and Economic Domination in Uganda
Christine Obbo

INTRODUCTION

In East Africa there co-exist two main views concerning women as biological and social reproducers and their membership within particular communities. On the one hand it is regarded as unimportant if one's mother, for example, is a foreigner as long as one has been successfully socialised according to the descent group ideology. It is held that the community gains through women marrying from one ethnic community into another. However, there is another view which perceives all women married to 'foreigners' as lost to the community. And by the same token women who marry into the community are perceived as being outsiders to the communities into which they marry. These contradictory views co-exist and are held by individuals often of the same group; they are more generally voiced by men who come from societies with a patrilineal descent system, as is the case usually in Uganda, although they exist as aspects of the dominant ideology which women hold also.

This chapter is concerned with the place of women's reproductive role in traditional ideologies defining 'the proper woman'.

Attitudes towards childless women, family planning and women's dress are indicators of the ways in which women's sexuality is defined and controlled. Arguments about scarce resources or foreign economic monopoly are often couched in terms of discussions about women and sexuality. The 'sexual protection' of women has a long history the world over and has a central place in patriotic discourses linked to nationalism and the defence of ethnic boundaries.

Both officially and privately ethnic chauvinism is regarded as mistaken and as a hindrance to Ugandan nationalism. However, sexism is treated as a given and therefore as unproblematic and natural: as specifying the commonsense existence of men and women. Differences between men and women are systematically and consistently emphasised to the detriment of women and as postulating subordination. This is evident in both public and private discussion and arguments represented in conversations that men have as well as those reported systematically in the media.

ISSUES AFFECTING WOMEN

In all Ugandan social or ethnic groups[1] women are defined primarily as reproducers of new group members; and as reproducers of social relations through their nurturing and socialisation roles. However, these important roles, which are regarded as paramount for social well-being, are used also as arguments to deny women a full and equal share in employment and access to social resources generally. Women's day to day lives are controlled and governed by a number of factors. First, internal societal or ethnic ideologies determine, on the one hand, the relationships between men and women through the systems of kinship and marriage; and on the other, the distribution of resources and access to resources and opportunities. Second, national policies regarding remuneration in employment (such as equal pay for equal work, or maternity and sick leave as well as other fringe benefits like car loans, housing, travel and vacations) benefit a minority of professional and educated women but leave the majority of employed women vulnerable to the whims of male employers and supervisors. There is no national policy or legislation protecting or offering a way to redress sexism at work. Third, government policies effectively benefit urban dwellers (mainly an elite minority) over and above the majority of workers in subsistence agriculture and the unskilled, unschooled urban migrants, most of whom are women. Fourth, Western influence has served to reinforce many of the internal social ideologies and has created new problems for women. For example, values concerning the 'good Christian wife' are rein-forced at high status levels by the importation of Victorian Christian teachings. Female emancipation and equality is preached but at the same time woman's place is seen as in the home and it is claimed that she should be pure, domestic and virginal. There is no doubt that the ideas about chastity found in both traditional and Christian ideologies serve to control women's sexuality. Again cash-crop farming and rural–urban migration were the direct result of foreign domination, foreign trade and generally the recent infiltration of a capitalist economy. Women have become the major agricultural producers of cash crops and food, and serve to sustain the national economy and subsidise the low urban wages paid to men. Needless to say, all this is rationalised in terms of 'mothers feeding their families'. Consequently when women migrate to towns they are often criticised and labelled as a 'wasted resource' because they are regarded as most needed in the rural areas.

The decree in 1973 regulating female attire asserted that Ugandan women should look dignified like 'our mothers', and was premised on the often voiced belief that women who wear tight or short dresses are morally loose. Urban women were coerced to obey the decree by mobs of men or by soldiers who were empowered to arrest and even enjoy sexual licence over such women. During the 1950s, 1960s and 1970s assumptions of moral looseness were definitely behind behaviour towards them, such as economic harassment, physical coercion, arrests and deportation to the rural areas. Often there was the added financial drain of having to pay court fines.

The ideological coercion is clear: women in the urban areas are forced to subsist on prostitution, thus devaluing their worth as 'mothers' in the public eye; women in the rural areas are 'good mothers' because they produce for subsistence through the labours of their hands. However, no woman wishes to be considered a bad woman, because this devalues her as a 'mother' in the eyes of her family and community. However, at issue is women's access to work in the urban areas, which migrants perceive as providing greater opportunities to improve their situation and enabling them to surmount the mere subsistence levels of the rural economy.

DOMINANT SOCIETAL IDEOLOGIES OF GENDER

All social groups in Uganda are organised according to patrilineal principles which give men dominance in marriage and property relations. Women's biological role as child-bearers is regarded as their primary social role and defines their social worth. Consequently most women want an unlimited number of children, but in practice may only have a few due to their fertility levels or the antenatal and postnatal survival chances of their children. However, some women want only a few children either because they suffer unduly during pregnancies and deliveries, or because they do not want to be aged by the constant bearing of children. Highly educated mothers generally want fewer children, whom they can support and educate well. Again, from all available evidence, a woman with one or two children is regarded as a 'one-eyed person' deserving pity, and a woman with no children is pitied for her misfortune in 'being barren', and is despised. These attitudes are strong even in areas like Buganda where the fertility levels are low and infertility not uncommon, due to dietary deficiencies and the impact of venereal disease.

Ugandan men from all societal groups and socio-economic levels want proof of a woman's fertility[2] (Molnos 1973). Pre-marital pregnancies occur among both uneducated girls who give in to male pressure and educated girls and women who may be living with their boyfriend, often in the hope of speeding up matrimony. Thus women's strategies as they negotiate their roles as women, and as full members of their societies, find them by and large conforming to dominant values about women's roles. Women find themselves in a double bind, concurrently trying to prove that their chastity is beyond reproach and that they will prove faithful to their husbands; and at the same time having to show their desirability as marriage partners through demonstrating their reproductive potential. Men of course continue to practise the double standard according to which they not only enjoy sexual relations before marriage but as married men have access to other men's wives and daughters.

Women's handling of the double bind in their lives and the double standards practised by men often reflects their social and economic position. Status-conscious women or those with high economic status will behave in different ways from women with low 'status', and will tend to turn a blind eye to their husbands' infidelities, although they will often develop a passionate dislike for the 'other woman' whom they regard as 'home wreckers' and 'bad women' generally. In this way, high status women become trapped by the ideology of the 'good woman' as a faithful wife and mother. The high status women contrast their moral uprightness with the improbity of the other 'bad women'. They fail to take account of the uneven distribution of resources and power between men and women; and between the privileged educated few and the unprivileged masses who are constantly striving to transcend this condition. Of course, it is not uncommon (although ideologically upholding the ideas of chastity) for elite women to have affairs with elite men.

RESOURCES AND PRODUCTION

Land ownership is the most important asset for all Ugandans, irrespective of cultural and socio-economic position. Even in pastoral societies where livestock ownership is the most visibly important economic resource, it goes without saying that one needs access to land in order to feed the animals. The issue of land ownership is particularly important to women because they see it as the passport to other societal resources. In nearly all Ugandan societies women had, and still have, access to land by virtue of being wives and mothers. Women as wives are expected to assist, or as some see it, to work for, their husbands. This is repeatedly revealed when women identify men as managers and controllers of the household labour force and women as the controlled labourers who have to budget their time in order to fulfil their duties as mothers, wives and producers as well as responsible citizens whose duty is to attend the sick and bereaved. Women who fulfil their roles as mothers, i.e. reproducers of the community, fare better than those women who do not. But the numbers of women who reject marriage have increased as women have gained greater access to land and other sources of incomes. However, all things being equal, women would rather have both economic security and marriage; but only elite women seem relatively successful in maintaining the balance. Women are generally critical of other women who are taken in by the male declaration that they have joint property ownership. The difficulties that divorced or widowed women face in overcoming the social and economic disadvantages and even dispossession that often beset them are well known. It is commonly agreed by both men and women that the poorest man in Uganda is one who has no female relative or wife to work for him. In relation to this, a hotly debated issue is the effect to the household economy if women were allowed ownership of land (or among pastoralists, cattle). It is generally believed that women would be more likely to abandon their husbands, 'what then would be the purpose of marriage if women controlled their own land or property?'[3] This brings out clearly that women are dependent upon marriage for economic survival given their lack of land ownership and access to other valuable economic resources. In the Buganda province of southern Uganda since 1900 it has been possible for the female relatives of powerful men to acquire individual freehold ownership rights through receiving gifts or purchasing land. Needless to say, rich women can gain access to more land than poor women. In a number of districts a few forceful women have gained access to land by applying to district boards. However, by and large rural women have increased their share in societal resources by using their contribution to subsistence production as the bargaining point.

The incorporation of Uganda into the international capitalist system had the effect of increasing female employment through the addition of cash crops to subsistence production. This is crucial to understanding the low ability of employers in the towns to pay wages to men, particularly those from labour-exporting regions. Most of these men had wives who acted as unpaid agricultural workers, and the state has quietly incorporated them into the economy as unpaid workers who have functioned to subsidise low urban male wages. The colonial government regarded African men as urban 'visitors' whose rightful place was in the rural areas. Social scientists have tended to label the migrants as 'target' workers – e.g. spending a few months or a year working to buy a bicycle, a cow or a sewing machine or to build a tin roofed house, and then returning to the rural areas. In reality the migrants alternated their urban employment with home leaves which allowed them to continue existing social and property relationships in the village and to conceive children. By the mid-1950s, social scientists regarded them as 'circulating' migrants; and by the mid-1960s as the heads of two-household families who shuttled between town and country.

During the 1960s the five-year plan of the independent government of Uganda advocated employment opportunities that would improve the lives of rural dwellers and thus bridge the gap between rural and urban real incomes. In other words the government was aware of the need to alleviate rural poverty, unemployment and underemployment if people were to stay in the rural areas. Yet in their rhetoric, government ministers treated the urban migrants as lazy rustics who had inadvertently drifted to the towns and who therefore should be returned to the land for gainful employment.

However, in all these attempts to define and understand the urban migrants, the discussion centred on men who were assumed to be the major 'breadwinners'. Women, who remained in the rural areas, generating a second income through cash-crop production, and ensuring that the migrants and the children were well fed and in good health, were rarely mentioned. The women found themselves in a double bind, on the one hand producing within a capitalist system for which they received no remuneration; and on the other hand subjected to an ideology that regarded land as a resource that belonged to men. Furthermore, urban policies and public stereotypes clearly spelled out the view that migration to towns was not appropriate for women.

SEX AND NATIONALISM

Women's 'security' is often the last frontier men have to defend when all the other battles against colonialism and imperialism are lost. Human societies always portray their women as more virtuous than women of other groups and therefore in need of protection. Never mind that each society also coerces women to be 'good women' through imposing a number of sanctions against 'bad women'. Sexual involvement with foreign men, for example, makes a woman 'bad'. In Africa generally and Uganda in particular such involvement is seen as a perpetuation of colonialism and imperialism: that is both as a form of cultural–political and economic domination. On the other hand women are expected to submit to the sexual advances of indigenous men who dominate political and economic life. Thus men in the modern African state reserve the right to specify and control women's sexuality in much the same way as found in the more traditional relations of Ugandan society. The following section will treat in detail the following: first, Idi Amin's attempt to reconstitute the 'authentic Ugandan woman' during the 1970s; and second, an episode from the 1940s nationalistic struggles against Asian commercial monopoly which indicates the links between nationalism and gender.

In 1972 when Idi Amin was consolidating his control over various sections of Uganda, he legislated as a popular measure that women had to wear long dresses, i.e. well below the knees and preferably ankle-length. Women who normally wore the long traditional garbs (Kikoyi, Ssuka or buluti) joined men in criticising those wearing Western-style dress, mainly women who were in gainful employment in the towns, usually educated women of professional status. This controversy revealed many areas of clash in Ugandan society. Thus women stood opposed to women – an essential element of the criticism here related to the abandonment of traditional folk ways and culture. In addition, highly educated women and wives of elite men in general also condemned those women who dressed 'indecently' in order to trap men. This was an obvious reference to those women in the supporting or service jobs such as secretaries, bank tellers, shop assistants and barmaids whose wages were inadequate and who were always at the receiving end of sexual advances from their bosses. Some women in this group may have found it necessary to supplement their wages by acquiring a lover to pay their rent: and still many others found it imperative to entertain their male superiors in order to keep their jobs or earn promotions. Thus professional or elite women who themselves faced sexual harassment at work, but were more able to deal with it, were critical of the less educated professional women who were seen as 'loose' and out to seduce, 'snatch the purses' of or 'steal' their husbands. In other words, when it came to competing for men, elite women found it convenient to ignore the first-hand knowledge of sexual harassment which sometimes operates to deny promotions.

The whole matter of dress was an indicator of how much control not only Amin but Ugandan men in general had over women. During a meeting convened by Amin to talk with women leaders, elite women initially wholly supported his legislation dictating women's dress and condemning 'bad women' who dressed 'indecently'. But as the meeting progressed they found themselves on the defensive. This happened when Amin claimed that some Uganda women were doing 'terrible things', i.e. practising prostitution with the Europeans at the Kenyan port of Mombasa and thus ruining the name of Uganda. While no one could emphatically deny that there were Ugandan prostitutes at Mombasa, the leaders of the women's group found it necessary to inform Amin that some of those women were in fact married to Europeans. Subsequently, their spokesperson and later minister and ambassador was accused of misusing government funds to buy jewellery, and then of engaging in sexual activity with an unknown European at Orly Airport in France. Amin's ultimate act of cutting her down to size was achieved by publishing alleged nude pictures of the minister when she was a top Vogue magazine model living abroad. In the logic of the moment, it did not matter that she was wearing body stockings. What was at issue was that she had exposed her body to a white photographer and who knows what else! The connection was being made in the public perception that a woman who undresses for foreign men – for whatever purpose – is a prostitute. The identification of non-conformist women in the area of dress and behaviour with prostitutes reached a head. The minister was put under house arrest and according to reliable sources, her waist-long hair was chopped off with broken bottles. According to those who were familiar with the circumstances it was her refusal to submit to Amin's sexual demands that led to this brutal treatment. Thus women must not only be willing to admit to the sexual advances of powerful men but they must not get involved with foreign men who represent colonialism and economic exploitation.

This point is best illustrated by a letter written in 1956 as part of the early nationalistic struggle against British colonialism and Asian commercial dominance. The letter is significant because it appeared in a vernacular newspaper intended for African not Asian or European readers. It expressed grievances against economic exploitation in general and the sexual exploitation of women in particular:

(a) . . . 'parasites' which suckle Uganda . . . rob us and make us poor . . . the Indian traders . . . are a millstone weighing many pounds around the neck of Africans . . . They trick us and rob us saying that they are selling goods to us reasonably at proper prices whereas in fact they are profiteering. (b) They employ our young children, boys and girls, at very low wages in fact the shs 2/ which is given to them does not suffice to obtain a shirt or frock to help them out of difficulties which have induced them to work. As a result the boys learn pick-pocketing and the girls become prostitutes. Also the Indians are responsible for these young girls taking up the profession. For instance, look at the number of mulattos or people with mixed color and the majority of them belong to the Indians of Uganda. What causes this mixture is their desire to enrich themselves. The result is nothing but misery because these mulatto children have nothing to help them, neither do they leave them anything when they go back to India, even though when they go back they have amassed a great deal of money from this country. (c) The personal servants and the people who work for the Indians are people who are always found to be exceedingly dirty and untrustworthy. It is amongst them that we find ignorant people who speak in an obscene manner and who have not the manners of polite people. This therefore shows that they are not fellows and they copy this from their masters, the Indians. The personal servants and also employees of some Europeans are found however, to be paid good wages and are also clever, and clean at the same time. (G.R. Kizza, April 1946; quoted in Low 1971: 131–2)

This letter raises many pertinent issues regarding nationalism, racism and women's sexuality. Whereas earlier letter writers had deplored Asian economic exploitation and their patronising attitudes (Z.K. Sentongo, July 1941; quoted in Low 1971: 54). This letter also condemns Asians as uncouth and irresponsible. It is not clear whether little girls were initiated into sex to supplement their poor wages or whether once initiated they were employed specifically for sexual services. Amongst other things the point of the letter seems to be that the Asians were not only encroaching upon the economic rights of African men but upon their sexual rights as well. What seems clear is that the penetration of capitalism had pushed people to seek labour in an Asian-controlled place. It was part of Pax Britannica to use buffer zones. The African chiefs served as the political buffer of indirect rule while the Asian traders were the economic buffer between the colonialists and the 'natives'. The letter is very positive about Europeans as employers and as people whose cleanliness and manners were presumably faultless and imparted to their employees.[4] However, the Indians are seen as the opposite, presumably because they are in close contact with the 'natives' whom they despise and feel free to abuse verbally or sexually. Elkan found in the industrial town of Jinja that men objected to women's employment in factories because they would be at risk of bearing half-caste children through sexual relations with Asian employers (Elkan 1956: 1–6).

It is important at this point to backtrack and outline the economic and political context of the letter. In East Africa (Kenya Colony, Uganda Protectoratate and Tanganyika Territory), colonial society was organised like a three-tiered pyramid. At the top were the Europeans who controlled the political economy; in the middle were their protégés, the Asian civil servants and traders and at the bottom were the Africans, referred to as 'natives'. There was another group mentioned in the letter, the mulattos or 'half-castes'. Such children were reared in all three colonial social tiers depending on how the Asian or European fathers felt about their offspring. It would seem that those raised in African homes found total acceptance. Those raised by European fathers with the help of all-white boarding schools in England or Kenya, and African *ayahs* ('nursemaids') exhibited the most confusion. This was due to the conflict between their experiences of racism against people of colour (i.e. not quite white) and the fact that their holidays were spent with African domestics (among whom may have been their mothers) whom they had learned to despise. In the colonial social ranking system, the half-castes were ranked below the Asians. But in the zone where the Arabs seemed to float half-castes were ranked in descending order, after Europeans, Asians and Arab. (At least that was the ranking in colonial boarding schools.) The Europeans felt most guilty about their half-castes, although they would not fully accept them in their community. When Uganda attained political independence in 1962 colonial and neo-colonial cultural imperialism was blatantly promoted by the 'friends of Uganda', as the ex-colonials and new arrivals called themselves. The Ugandan Asian continued business as usual and still controlled the theatre and newspapers which were important vehicles for the dissemination of so-called 'cultural information' in the urban areas. One incident stands out clearly. When in 1962 Uganda, for the first time ever, entered a Miss World beauty contest, a half-caste with a European father was selected as Miss Uganda. Her confusion surfaced in London during press conferences when she claimed that her father was a rich coalminer. No coal has yet been discovered in Uganda and the girl's father was a civil servant.

CONCLUDING REMARKS: SEX AND POWER

In the final analysis, the racial tiering reflects the political economy and the relationships it generated. Property generally divides people into exploiters and exploited. Capitalist ideology stresses the freedom of individuals to sell their labour, but obscures the limited choices people have, which makes such freedom difficult, and the facts of exploitation. The colonial economic structure is the basic agent of change in relation to other social institutions. The employment of young children and particularly the sexual exploitation of girls is a case in point.

The issues of controlling or exploiting women's sexuality is a recurrent theme in relation to women's employment. As late as the 1960s, the employment of girls and women, though regarded as necessary in some cases, was seen as problematic. Salaried men often stopped the employment of qualified wives because 'their bosses will seduce them'. Uneducated men, whose wives worked for wages, bitterly resented the elite who controlled access to opportunities and employment, appropriating the sexual services of their wives. Ambitious, unmarried and salaried men all insist that they wish to marry women who will work and earn. However, these same men, as well as those with non-working wives or those who resent their wives' working, claim that women obtain and maintain jobs through being sexually accessible or that women take away jobs from men who are more deserving of work.

The argument presented in this chapter is that women's biological reproductive role has been used in debates about nationalism and those concerned with the need to control women. McKinnon has argued that 'Marxism and feminism are theories of power and its unequal distribution. They provide accounts of how social arrangements of patterned disparity can be internally rational yet unjust.

They argue, respectively, that the relations in which many women work and a few gain, in which some fuck and others get fucked are the prime moments of politics' (MacKinnon 1982: 156, 517). However, in all political moments the available options determine people's strategies. Women's conscious or unwitting choices often serve to reproduce and reinforce attitudes and practices in which their sexuality and its control are used by men to abuse them, to deny them certain privileges and to symbolically pursue struggles. In summary, this chapter has indicated that Uganda is predominantly a man's world in which sexuality – 'that social process which creates, organizes, expresses and directs desire, creating social beings we know as women and men, as their relations create society' (MacKinnon 1982: 516) – like other domains of society is controlled by men who reserve the right to dictate what women's sexuality should be. Patriotic arguments in defence of nationalism or ethnic boundaries incorporate in a central way notions of women's sexuality both in terms of sex and biological reproduction.

NOTES

1. The information presented in this paper was gathered between 1971 and 1974, and has been updated through subsequent letters and short-period research in 1977.
2. Ideas surrounding female sexuality and fertility in select East African societies have been adequately covered in Molnos (1973). The Ugandan groups covered in the volumes include the Baganda (Mere N. Kisekka; Martin Southwold); the Nyoro (John Beattie); the Lugbara (John F. Middleton); the Lango (Richard R. Curley); the So (Charles S. Laughlin and E.R. Laughlin); the Jie (John E. Lamphear); the Kiga (Rachel Van der Meeren-Yeld); and the Nkole (Musa T. Mushanga).
3. Co-operative officer during a discussion following a lecture given by the author on 19 May 1983 to 20 co-operative officers from Uganda at the University of Winsconsin-Madison.
4. The writer of the letter was a Mugandan. The Gandan maintained ethnic boundaries by claiming that everyone who was like Europeans was dirty and not like them. For example, this argument was used when they demanded separate hospital wards at Mulago. The argument also came up constantly during my fieldwork as an explanation of why Nyoro or Ruandan women were unacceptable as marriage partners. But since there were Gandan men married to Nyoro and Ruandan women, the explanation for this was: 'She is practically like us! She has

learned to be clean.' It is therefore alright having a Nyoro mother as long as she bears you in the clan (*Nyoko aberanga Munyolo nakuzaala Mukikka*). With regard to the Asians, most Ugandans groups considered them dirty because they spat in public, blew their noses using their bare hands and loudly cleared their mucus in their noses and swallowed it.

BIBLIOGRAPHY

Elkan, Walter (1956) 'The Employment of Women in Uganda', mimeo 1–6. Also published in *Bulletin de l'Insitut inter African du Travail, Brazzaville*, vol. 4 (1957) no. 4, 8–23.

Low, D.A. (1971) *The Mind of Buganda: Documents of the Modern History of an African Kingdom* (London: Heinemann).

MacKinnon, Catherine A. (1982) 'Feminism, Marxism, Method and the State: an Agenda for Theory', *Signs* vol. 7 (Spring) 516–17.

Molnos, Angela (1973) 'Cultural Source Materials for Population Planning', in Angela Molnos (ed.), *East Africa: vol. 3, Beliefs and Practices* (Nairobi: East Africa).

6 National Reproduction and 'the Demographic Race' in Israel

Nira Yuval-Davis

The issue of national reproduction in Israel, both in terms of its ideological boundaries and in terms of the reproduction of its membership, has always been at the centre of zionist discourse. During the 1980s, however, it has gradually come to overshadow even the issue of security as a precondition for Israel's survival. However, Golda Meir, the prime minister of Israel at the time, already confided in the early 1970s that she was afraid of a situation in which 'she would have to wake up every morning wondering how many Arab babies have been born during the night'! (quoted in Kahane 1983: 52).

A 'demographic race' between Jews and Arabs in Israel is seen as crucial to the survival of Israel, not only as the state apparatus of the population living in it, but as the state for Jews everywhere. Revealingly, the official aim of the Israeli demographic centre which was established as a unit attached to the Israeli prime minister's office in April 1967, is 'to act systematically to realize a demographic policy directed at creating an atmosphere and conditions for encouraging a higher birth rate, which is so vital to the future of the *Jewish people*' (my emphasis – NY-D; Demographic Centre 1979: 1).

This statement has to be read whilst bearing in mind that more than 75 per cent of world Jewry, according to statistics produced by that same demographic centre, live outside Israel. On the other hand, 17 per cent of Israeli citizens and about a third of the people under the direct control of the Israeli government (including those living in the territories occupied by Israel since 1967) are not Jews.

Israel was established for a specific purpose, and as the achievement of a specific political movement – zionism. While, as most of the chapters in this volume reveal, the definition of boundaries of national collectivities and their relationship to the state is very often problematic, in Israel it is especially so.[1] This can be understood partly in terms of the specific historical construction of the Jewish people as a territoryless people/caste with a religious civilisation in which Palestine was regarded as the 'land of the Fathers' and 'the Promised Land'. Like many other ethnic collectivities in Europe and particularly in the Third World, the dichotomy of nation/religion has not suited the historical construction of the Jewish people. Zionism has been only one response, and for a very long time a minority one, of the Jews in the 'modern' world to this history; in particular to their displacement and persecution with the rise of capitalism and nationalism in Europe in which their traditional mode of existence could not survive any longer (Leon 1970; Halevi 1986). The zionist movement aspired to the 'normalisation' of the Jewish people, through the establishment of a Jewish state in an independent territory in which, ideally, all Jews would eventually settle. The problems of defining the boundaries of the Israeli national collectivity stem, therefore, not only from the specific character of the Jewish people, but are also a result of the history of zionist settlement in Palestine and the establishment of a settler colonial society there. This relates to contradictions in Israeli social structures and social forces, in relation to Jews outside Israel and non-Jews within Israel, as well as ethnic, religious and class divisions amongst Israeli Jews themselves. All of these contradictions are expressd in debates in Israel around demographic issues.

Demographic policies often seem to be determined by worries over sufficient labour power for the national economy. Indeed the literature on reproduction often assumes it to be the complementary facet to economic production, or rather a precondition to it (e.g. Edholme *et al*; 1976 McIntosh 1981). A closer examination of national demographic policies (as well as state welfare policies), however, will often reveal that national political rather than economic interests lie behind the desire to have more children, or rather, more children of a specific origin.[2] In Israel, where economistic calculations have never seriously determined major political decisions (even in the heart of an extremely economic crisis (Yuval-Davis 1984), this is certainly the case. This chapter will therefore concentrate on examining the nationalist angle in the ideological debates and policies which have surrounded the question of the birth rate in Israel. It will then consider the ways in which the political and ideological pressures to define and reproduce the national collectivity in Israel have constituted Israeli Jewish women as its national reproducers.

DEMOGRAPHIC POLICIES AND THE 'NEED' FOR A JEWISH MAJORITY

Israeli demographic policies have had two hegemonic goals:

(a) the first has been to maintain and, if possible, increase Jewish domination in Israel, both in terms of a numerical majority and also in terms of military and technological superiority over the Arabs;

(b) the second one, which gradually plays a more and more central role in the preoccupation of the Israeli policy makers, has been to reproduce and enlarge 'the Jewish people' all over the world and for Israeli Jewish mothers to have enough children to 'compensate' for the children lost in the Nazi Holocaust and to what is called in Israel the 'Demographic Holocaust' and assimilation.

Traditionally, as a settler society, immigration (*Aliya*) was considered to be both the quickest as well as the cheapest and most efficient method of increasing the Jewish zionist presence in Palestine. The 'need' for a Jewish majority has always been the cornerstone in zionist thinking. Ben-Gurion, debating in the *Knesset* (the Israeli parliament) in 1949 (during the war which expanded Israel's territory far beyond the territory allocated to it by the UN), explained:

A Jewish state . . . even if only in the west of Palestine is impossible, if it is to be a democratic state, because the number of Arabs in the western part of Palestine is higher than that of the Jews . . . we want a Jewish state, even if not all over the country. (Protocols of the Knesset, 4 April 1949)

The priority of a Jewish majority in Israel in zionist strategy has been one of the issues debated all along between the 'left' and 'right' of the zionist movement, especially before the establishment of the state and after 1967. A Jewish majority has always been more important to the zionist 'left'. However, even the zionist 'left' was prepared to accept a majority of only 55 per cent in the first instance, as was planned in the UN partition plan of 1947 which was to divide Palestine into a Jewish and Palestinian state (this never actually materialised as a result of the 1948 war). The zionist 'left', however, planned various ways to expand that majority (Bailin 1985).

During the 1948 war, Israel enlarged by more than 50 per cent its allocated territory, having divided the planned Palestinian state with

Jordan. This could have meant a Jewish state with an overwhelming Palestinian majority. However, most of the Palestinians under Israeli rule either escaped during the battles and were never allowed to return, or were expelled by force. This, plus the major Jewish immigration, in its first few years of existence, to Israel from postwar Europe and from the Arab countries, reduced the Palestinian minority in Israel in the early 1950s to no more than 11 per cent. Still, in the hope of reinforcing this ration, Ben-Gurion initiated in the early 1950s rewards (of IL100 – even then more of symbolic than substantial value) for 'herione mothers', defined as those who have had ten children or more. Israeli Jewish mothers continued to be urged to have more children.

The birth rate within the Jewish and Palestinian population in Israel was not, however, even. In the early 1960s the situation arose whereby, on the one hand mass Jewish immigration to Israel stopped, and on the other hand the rate of birth also started to drop amongst the more traditionally oriented Israeli Jews. At the same time, the Palestinian birth rate in Israel did not decrease significantly, while Palestinians' life expectancy increased (by 1967 the Arab minority in Israel constituted 15 per cent in comparison with the 11 per cent of the early 1950s).

The 'ultimate threat' of the gradual growth of the Palestinian community in Israel and the 'erosion of the Jewish majority' kept on growing as a political issue, especially after the 1967 war and the public debate about annexation of the occupied territories with its massive Palestinian population. But the concern has been growing also in relation to the Palestinians who live within the 1949 borders, who are Israeli citizens, and who, for the first time in the 1980s started to be counted, for sheer numbers, as an important electorate lobby.[3]

In the mid-1960s (before the 1967 war and around the time of the establishment of the demographic centre), major confiscations of Arab lands were carried out in the Galillee. The official name of this policy, initiated by Levy Eshkol, the prime minister at the time, was to 'Judaise Galillee'. When this goal failed a public debate developed, triggered by a secret document leaked to the press which was written in 1967 by a civil officer called Konig. Various means were suggested to fight this tendency, which included, among others, encouraging Arab emigration from the country by limiting Arab prospects of employment and studies, cutting Arab child national insurance benefits and more. Since then, the 'demographic race' and the annual Jewish and Arab birth rate continue to be discussed prominently in the Israeli national press, accompanied by gloomy demographic predictions and/or attempts to refute them.

The Israeli Palestinians have not been reluctant participants in the 'demographic race'. Large numbers of children, especially boys, has always been important in Arab rural society, which was organised around the extended family. Modernisation has had contradictory short term effects on the rate of growth of the population. The rate of life expectancy has grown; the rate of mortality has fallen, and both these facts have overwhelmed the beginning of the trend of falling birth rates (Ronen 1982).

Since the 1970s the number of children has become also a conscious political weapon among Palestinian nationalists. This has been true about the whole of the Palestinian movement. In the 'post-Konig report' period, slogans like 'The Israelis beat us at the borders but we beat them at the bedrooms' started to be heard, and poems, a traditional mobilising means in Arab societies, were written in this spirit.[4] The Israeli authorities more or less admitted that no active policies of population control which are used in other Third World countries have any chance of finding co-operation from either the 'traditional' or the 'modern' elements in the Arab sector. Nevertheless, social welfare clinics were established, and Palestinian women are the only ones in Israel who can obtain free contraceptives.[5]

Since the Israeli government is unable effectively to control the number of Palestinian children being born, quite a lot of Israeli government policies have concentrated on bringing more Jews from abroad and gradually, when that happened less and less, promoting and encouraging the growth of the Jewish birth rate in Israel itself. This was done both through propaganda work and with material incentives. For example, 'The Fund of Encouraging Birth' was established in 1968 by the Housing Ministry to subsidise housing loans for families with more than three children. These benefits, like larger child allowances, were given basically only to Jews, under the euphemistic definition of 'families who have relatives who have served in the Israeli army'.

Clearly all these policies have been of greater symbolic than of practical value when we take into consideration what is actually involved in bringing up a child. But even on this symbolic and auxiliary–practical level, these policies were not universally approved of in Israel.

One line of objection was raised by militant liberals and leftists.

They joined the Israeli Palestinians in pointing out the racist character of using the state apparatus to discriminate against Palestinians
and to block their access to a whole line of state benefits. Right wing
nationalists, however, also objected to using the state apparatus for
that purpose – they would have preferred the Jewish Agency, which
caters only for Jews and not for all Israeli citizens.

Another line of opposition to these policies was on the grounds
that, while promoting national goals, these policies were not taking
into account class (and therefore also intra-Jewish ethnic) divisions in
the Israeli society – as the number of children rather than the income
of the family was used as the qualifying criterion for child and housing
benefits.

This line of opposition reflected a growing concern in the early
1970s with issues of poverty and ethnic antagonism within the Jewish
collectivity. Class differentiations between Ashkenazi (of Occidental
origin) and Oriental (mostly of Arab countries origin) Jews in Israel
grew rather than shrunk in the 1960s (Smooha 1978; Bernstein and
Svirsky). This situation changed somewhat in the 1970s through the
influx of a large number of Palestinians from the occupied territories
into the Israeli labour market and the consequent economic upward
mobility of sections of the Oriental Jews. Nevertheless, the Jewish
poor in Israel today are still overwhelmingly of Oriental Jewish origin
(E. Farjun; A. Ehlich 1983). Growing popular protest movements
within what is often called 'The Second Israel' (the best known one
but by no means the only one being the Israeli Black Panthers) have
brought this reality to the political arena as well, especially as the
Oriental Jews have become the majority of the Israeli electorate.

The government committee which examined these issues found
that 75 per cent of the children who grew up in Israel in economic
deprivation have come from large families of four-plus children,
mostly from Oriental Jewish families, and they constitute about 40
per cent of all Israeli children (Prime Minister's Committee
1974).

It is important to note in this context that, although a Jewish
majority in Israel was very important to the zionist movement, it was
also always very aware that in the Arab east it will always be a very
small minority. The petit bourgeois socio-economic background of
most of the zionist settlers before the establishment of the state, their
technological and organisational superiority over the underdeveloped
Arab world, imperialist support as the most consistent local allies and
the nationalist myth of 'there is no alternative', all enabled the

continuous success of Israel in its wars against the Arabs (at least until the Lebanon War). Quality, then, rather than quantity was the crucial factor. (In the late 1970s and 1980s the situation has been changing and Israeli newspapers reported with anxiety that there is a much higher number of university graduates in the Arab world than in Israel as well as a growing deterioration in the quality of the Israeli army human power (e.g. Sharit 1985).

It was therefore, again, primarily a national concern, as well as an attempt to appease the growing protests of 'Second Israel' (as the Oriental Jews are frequently known), which affected a significant development in the direction of welfare policies in Israel in the 1970s, measures such as the introduction of social security, 'slum rehabilitation' programmes etc. For a while the (Jewish) family's economic situation rather than the number of children became the official criterion for housing support.

This political trend, resulting from the fear of too many children growing up in poverty-stricken households in Israel, can also be said to be one of the major factors which, combined with ideological pressures, have brought about abortion legislation in Israel. This occurred after years when there were no official policies on abortion, which had resulted from the fear of running into political trouble whatever decisions would be taken (Yishai 1978). In fact, abortion legislation has become one of the major mobilisation factors of the growing right wing nationalist and religious camp. For them, not only abortions but family planning in general for families smaller than four children is objectionable.[6]

For large sections in the pro-natal lobby in Israel, having many children is not just an inevitable outcome of keeping religious codes concerning procreation, an expression of Jewish traditional values or even a means of making Israel stronger by enlarging the number of potential soldiers. It is not even a question of simply keeping a Jewish majority in Israel. It is also a way of reproducing and enlarging the Jewish people which has dwindled, first through the Nazi Holocaust (caused by anti-semitism) and then through the 'Demographic Holocaust' (caused by assimilation and intermarriage when there is not enough anti-semitism).[7]

If, at the beginning of the zionist endeavour, it was the Jewish mothers in the Diaspora who produced human power for the Yishuv settlement in Palestine, it was now the 'duty' of the Israeli Jewish mothers to produce even more children for the sake of the Jewish people as a whole. In 1983 the 'Law on Families Blessed with

Children' was passed, giving a whole range of subsidies to families with more than three children.

The lobby which organised the pro-natal politics in the early 1980s revived the 'Efrat committee for the encouragement of a higher Jewish birth rate' which had been dormant for most of the 1970s. In the early 1980s it became powerful enough to establish centres and branches all over the country. It was able to incorporate within its ranks major elite figures from all professional fields, both religious and secular, and to gain an official place as a governmental consultative body on natal and demographic policies committees (together with the official women's organisations). Efrat gained much of its public power through linking the debate on the Jewish birth rate with the public campaign around the abortion issue.

As part of its coalition agreement with the religious parties, the Begin government, when it came to power in the late 1970s, abolished the one category in the abortion law which enabled legal abortions to be carried out on the grounds of 'social hardships' (the other categories are: the age of the woman; the pregnancy being a result of 'forbidden relations'; health of the fetus; and health of the woman). This angered the feminist lobby, but was not enough to appease the anti-abortion lobby, especially as liberal social workers on the abortion committees have tended to apply the woman's health category instead.[8] Along with the usual reasoning of anti-abortion lobbies who treat abortions as murders came the emotive call to the Jewish mothers to do their national duty and replace the Jewish children killed by the Nazis. An extreme example of this ideology was a suggestion, narrowly defeated, of the Advisor of the Minister of Health of the time, Haim Sdan, to force every woman considering abortion to watch a slide show which would include, in addition to horrors of dead fetuses in rubbish bins, the pictures of dead children in Nazi concentration camps. After a large public campaign this specific proposal was defeated and Sdan eventually resigned. Nevertheless, 'the war on the demographic war' continues.

It is worth remarking, however, that at the time of writing this chapter, in the mid-1980s, the effects of the overall economic, political and ideological crisis in Israel were making their marks on the various policies which have been used in the 'demographic race'. Within an overall context of drastic cuts in real wages and the threat of rising unemployment, the effectively reduced state incentives have lost, to a great extent, any practical effects that they might have had a few years previously. This, plus a growing negative balance of immigration and emigration movements to and from the country, have gradually turned attention more and more to the transfer of Palestinians from the country, as the only possible valid long-term solution for keeping the zionist character of the Israeli state.[9]

Nevertheless, on January 1986 Avidov-Hacohen MP, of the Likud Party, suggested making 1987 an official year for 'the encouragement of Jewish birth rate in Israel'. Hooting and laughter followed his speech in the Knesset from its more liberal and leftist members and wonderful satires followed in the press. But his suggestion has had enough support not to be defeated. One of the Knesset committees received the task of promoting this proposal as part of its agenda.

JEWISH WOMEN AND 'THE NATION'

We have seen how Israeli Jewish women have been 'recruited' in the 'demographic war' to bear more children as their national duty to the Jewish people in general and in the Israeli Jewish people in particular. It is debatable to what extent the ideological pressures, child benefits or other formal and material collective measures are the crucial factors for having a child, or when an unplanned pregnancy occurs, for keeping it. The emotional needs of people in a permanent war society (when husbands and sons might get killed at any moment) and cultural familial traditions probably play a much more central role than anything else. Whatever the main reason, the fact is that Israeli Jewish women, especially professional middle class women, do bear more children than their counterparts in other advanced capitalist societies.[10] And their role as suppliers of children to 'the nation' directly affects the availability of contraceptives and abortions. As mentioned before, there are no free contraceptives in Israel (except for Palestinians) and abortion legislation is a focus of major public political debates – not unique to Israel, but with a very explicit nationalistic emphasis in comparison with campaigns in other countries where the 'moral right' has been fighting against abortion legislation.

Historically – until the 1960s, and since the beginning of the zionist movement – it has been mainly Jewish mothers in the Diaspora who 'supplied' the human power for the zionist settlement to be possible. The zionist endeavour can be described as involving an organisation with clear international division of labour – in the Diaspora the members and supporters of the movement supplied financial and political support and human power, and in Palestine, at the 'front', these resources were used to promote the zionist project of establishing an exclusively Jewish society over Palestine (Hecht and Yuval-Davis 1978; A. Ehrlich 1980). This division of labour continues to date, as without the financial and political support of the Jewish Diaspora, Israel could not have continued to exist. In the supply of human material, however, the balance has gradually shifted and the discussion today focuses, as we have seen, on the role of Israeli Jewish mothers in replacing the overall shrinking Jewish national collectivity all over the world rather than, or in addition to, the other way around.

Within the zionist Yishuv itself, pressures were out on Israeli Jewish women to bear more children since the beginning of the limitation on the number of Jewish immigrants to Palestine under the British mandate.[11]

However, initially the main emphasis of Jewish motherhood in Israel had more to do with its qualitative aspect – of producing the 'New Jew', 'the Sabre', the antithesis of the 'Diaspora Jew' whose negative image the zionist movement shared with European anti-semitism – rather than necessarily with the quantity of children. The latter was envisaged as coming mainly from Jewish Aliya from abroad. The role of the Israeli woman was to participate in the national struggle, mainly in supportive roles (Yuval-Davis 1982; 1985), and in addition, to produce proud, rooted and 'normal' children.

The development of the specific ideological construction of women as national reproducers in Israel has had much to do with the specificity of the historical development of Israeli society as a permanent war society. The ideological placement of women in this respect was best summed up by M.P. Geula Cohen:

> The Israeli woman is an organic part of the family of the Jewish people and the female constitutes a practical symbol of that. But she is a wife and a mother in Israel, and therefore it is of her nature to be a soldier, a wife of a soldier, a sister of a soldier, a grand-mother of a soldier. This is her reserve service. She is continually in military service. (Hazelton 1978: 113)

There have been many myths concerning the role of Israeli women as soldiers (Yuval-Davis 1985). Basically, however, and to a great extent as in the civil labour market, women in the army serve in subordinate and supportive roles to that of men, unless in roles which directly correspond to the ideological tradition of women in looking after the welfare of their menfolk. The few women who are engaged in combative occupation do so in order to release men for front duties from which women soldiers are officially banned. Also, as Geula Cohen says, women, unlike men, are released mostly from reserve service which is the mass popular base of the Israeli army where men serve at least one month a year until they are 50 years old, as their most important national role. The women's national role then becomes to produce babies who would become soldiers in future wars.

This ideological construction can explain why groups like 'Women against the War' and 'Parents against Silence' have been so effective in their protest against the Lebanon War. They have touched the heart of the ideological assumption that the Israel Jewish society is fighting only because 'there is no other alternative' for continuous collective survival, and therefore the individual's sacrifices (constructed specifically according to gender and age and to a certain extent class and ethnic origin) are willingly made. When we look at the effects of the national reproductive role of Israeli Jewish women, however, it is important to remember that we are dealing here not only, and even not mainly, with effects which relate to the actual number of children they produce and for what. We are also concerned with the ideological and legal constraints in which this role of theirs is being constructed.

Jewish women in Israel, and for that matter in the Diaspora as well, are being incorporated actively in the zionist endeavour, not only in supplying humanpower to the national collectivity, but also legally and symbolically, as markers of its boundaries. A Jew, according to the Law of Return, which entitles any Jew from anywhere in the world to automatic citizenship in Israel, and following the Jewish orthodox religious law, is somebody who was born to a Jewish mother (unless s/he is a religious convert). Motherhood, therefore, rather than fatherhood determines membership in the collectivity.

However, this matrilineal tradition does not mean that Jewish society is a matriarchal one. It is not even fully matrilineal – as the family name of the child is that of her/his father, and not the mother. The collective matrilinearity in determining who is a Jew was suitable to the existence of the Jewish community as a persecuted minority, in which pogroms and rapes were historically a recurring phenomenon.

As such, motherhood was a safer way of determining inclusive boundaries, and tight measures were taken in the religious code to secure the legitimate reproduction of the boundaries of the Jewish collectivity marked by its women.

Jewish women in the Diaspora in principle can choose whether or not to remain subjugated to the religious code. Not so Israeli women. The Israeli state apparatus has added its coercive power to the traditional voluntary Jewish communal power in several crucial instances, and given it monopolistic rights. This requires explanation, as the zionist movement generally presented itself as a 'modern alternative' way of being Jewish to the traditional religious one. However, in spite of the fact that the majority of the zionists were, at least originally, vehement secularists the zionist movement never completely broke away from Jewish orthodoxy. The zionist movement needed the religious tradition for justifying its claim over Palestine as its homeland, rather than the land of its indigenous population; it also needed the recognition of at least major sections of the orthodox Jewish communities, as the zionist movement claimed to represent all the Jews all over the world.

This is why (in addition to more *ad hoc* government coalition calculations) there has always been a partial incorporation of the Jewish religious legislation into the Israeli state legislation and hence its usage for determination of 'who is a Jew'.

To be born Jewish is more than being a child of a Jewish mother. One has to be born to a Jewish mother in the 'proper' way – otherwise one is considered a *mamzer* ('bastard'), would not be considered a Jew, is not able even to become a Jew by conversion, and one's descendants cannot marry other Jews 'for ten generations'. Bastardy in Judaism is not a question of being born outside wedlock as sexual intercourse, according to Jewish religious law, is one of the ways marriage can be contracted (as long as it is another Jew – rapes during pogrom did not receive such a 'sanctification'). Bastardy is a question of being born to a woman who is having a forbidden relationship of adultery or incest – and that includes even women who are divorced by civil (rather than religious) court, which unlike civil marriages are not recognised by the religious court, and who are having children from their second husband.

The major ideological justification which has been given for the incorporation of orthodox religious personal law into Israeli legislation and accepting its definition of 'who is a Jew' has been that doing otherwise will 'split the people'. It was claimed that accepting the authority or other Jewish religious denominations, such as the Conservative and Reform Judaism, let alone secular legislation, would make it impossible for orthodox Jews to marry anyone but other orthodox Jews, for fear of incorporating unintentionally the forbidden mamzers into their family. The paradox is, of course, that in reality no orthodox Jew marries a non-orthodox one (or even newly 'born again' orthodox Jews who come from secular families – exactly because of this fear). Moreover, outside Israel the majority of Jews do marry and divorce in a non-orthodox fashion, even if they marry before a Rabbi, and in Israel itself private contracts in lawyers' offices have become more and more popular as an established alternative to official marriages. The attempt to control the Israeli collectivity boundaries and its patterns of reproduction in an homogeneous way by incorporating the severe orthodox religious law into the Israeli state legislation has, therefore, not really succeeded. On the other hand, it has had a fundamental influence on the position of women in Israel.

Several attempts have been made since the establishment of the state of Israel to guarantee equal rights for women in terms of employment and payments, as well as to protect their rights as workers when becoming mothers. This legislation suffers from limitations similar to other legislations found in this area in Western states, in which women are constituted in the law primarily as wives and mothers. Also as in other countries, this legislation does not manage to alter the basic segregation and inequality between women and men in the labour market (Land 1978; Wilson 1977). What is more specific to Israel, however, is the fact that all the attempts to guarantee women's overall equal constitutional rights in principle have failed. This was not so much the result of direct intervention by the religious parties, as that of preventative actions of the other zionist parties who were afraid of the withdrawal of the support of the religious parties from their coalition governments which would damage the zionist claim to be 'the representative of the Jewish people'. This is why Rabin, the Labour government prime minister in 1975, declared that a Fundamental (i.e. quasi-constitutional) Law of Women's Equality will never be passed in Israel. However, as early as the 1930s, at the height of its ideological zeal, the Labour zionist movement (which defined itself as secular) was ready to give up women's right to vote. This was in order to prevent withdrawal of the extreme religious communities from the Yishuv institutions (the zionist settler community). What 'saved' the women then was the fact that the extremist religious parties withdrew anyway (Azaryahu 1977).

Women do have the right to vote in Israel, although in the last few years they have been prevented from doing so in local elections in some extreme religious settlements, especially among the settlers in the occupied territories (like Immanuel). But in the 1950s, Golda Meir was prevented from becoming a candidate for the mayorship of Tel-Aviv as, according to the Halakha, it was claimed, 'women are not allowed to govern men' – and this position never changed. Golda herself was eventually 'allowed' to become prime minister because, it was argued, formally her role there was that of 'first among equals'.

The most serious effects of the incorporation of religious laws into state legislation on women's status relate to their position in family law, where control of their constitution as bearers of the national collectivity is most carefully guarded. They are not allowed to become judges in the orthodox Rabbinical state courts which have the monolopy to decide in issues of marriage and divorce, and their evidence as a rule is not accepted, especially if there are male witnesses. In relation to the guardianship of children and to maintenance, there are two parallel court authorities, secular and religious. In the latter, especially, constructions of what should be the proper duties of a wife are exclusively decided by a small reactionary patriarchal group of Rabbinical judges. If these 'duties' are to be unfulfilled they result in a woman losing all her maintenance rights and being declared 'a rebel'. The inequality between the sexes affects also the women whose husbands disappear – in peacetime and even more so in Israel's continuous wars. Unlike men, they are not allowed to remarry until some proof can be brought that their husbands are certainly dead, and if they move to live with another man and have children by him, the latter are declared as *mamzerim*, outsiders to the Jewish national collectivity for ever.

A CONCLUDING REMARK

This chapter has examined some of the factors determining the relationship between women's position and their roles in Israeli society and the central concern of zionism for the reproduction of the Israeli national collectivity as 'Jewish'. To this purpose it has focused on the series of debates accompanying various demographic policies which have attempted to reinforce it. It shows that issues of

marriage and divorce, birth control and child benefits are intimately
linked with claims over territories and citizenship rights, class divisions and plans of mass transfer.

The first proposal for a private Member of Parliament's Bill that
was raised by Rabbi Kahana, the leader of the neo-nazi Kach Party
was, therefore, no mere coincidence. Rabbi Kahana's party has been
the fastest growing political power in Israel in the last few years. He
preaches for the mass expulsion of Palestinians from all over Israel as
well as the occupied territories and a few years ago established in
Jerusalem the museum of 'the Future Holocaust', predicting an end
of American Jewry similar to that in Nazi Germany. His proposed
Bill (which was invalidated on legal grounds so as to avoid formal
voting on the issue in the Israeli parliament) suggested the legal
prohibition of sexual relations between Jewish women and Arab
men. Women and their sexuality are seen as the gate-keeping
elements for the boundaries of the national collectivity.

This leads directly to the question, to what extent feminist struggle
is possible within zionist discourse (Hecht and Yuval-Davis 1978;
Lehzman 1987). It is a sobering revelation in that respect to read an
editorial not by Kahana, but by the liberal zionist Uri Avner, one of
the most consistent fighters in Israel for democracy, civil rights and
women's equality. Avnery, who in the mid-1960s used to mock the
demographic-race mentality as 'rabbit psychology', states as an
acceptable fact in the mid-1980s that 'The new Jewish community in
this country, from the beginning of the Zionist Aliya until today,
simply cannot absorb anybody who is not Jewish' (*Haolam Hazeh*,
24 April 1985).

Are Kahana's supporters right when they claim that he is the most
consistent zionist?

NOTES

1. See part I of my paper 'The Jewish Collectivity and National Repro-
    duction in Israel' in *Khamsin 13, Women in the Middle East* (London:
    Zed Books, 1987). The present chapter is based on parts II and III of
    that paper.
2. See, for example, Beveridge Report (1942: 154): 'With its present rate
    of reproduction, the British race cannot continue; means of reversing
    the recent course of birth rate must be found.' And in the Soviet

Union, like in Israel, they rewarded 'herione mothers' for those with ten children and more (*Guardian*, March 1979).

3. During the last election campaign, for the first time the election campaign by the major zionist parties in the Arab sector in Israel did not take place mainly via traditional Hamula heads. This was especially true for the party headed by General Ezer Weizman.

4. In May 1976, the poet Owani Sawit was arrested after reading some of his poems in the 'Day of the Land' memorial, including a poem in which he promised: 'Hey murderer/ Do you really believe that you can murder my people?/ This is an impossible mission/ If you murder six, we shall bring to the world sixty on that same day' (Arabic).

5. I was told by a social worker, that as long as these clinics were headed by Palestinian women, they tended to co-operate with the Israeli authorities on policies of family planning, although from a very different motivation – of care for individual women rather than control of overall numbers. During the 1980s, Palestinian men have become heads of some of these clinics and it is rumoured that attitudes towards family planning have changed considerably.

6. The secretary of the Efrat committee explained to me that, as so many Jewish women get married and start bearing children only after their military service (at the age of 20), any family planning aimed at limiting child-bearing to once every few years would necessarily limit severely the number of children such women could have before menopause.

7. Professors Baki and Dela Pergulas of the Hebrew University are continually quoted in the press, predicting the shrinking of world Jewry from the present 11.5 million to 8 million by the year 2000 and to 5 million by the 2200, and pointing out that by now 43 per cent of world Jewry births are taking place in Israel (although less than 25 per cent of world Jewry actually live there).

8. The table in the Efrat bulletin (no. 15–16) shows that in 1979 there were 15 925 legal abortions in Israel, of which 1665 were granted under the category of the age of the women; 4465, forbidden relations; 2165, danger to the embryo; 1299, danger to the woman; and 6331, the social situation of the woman. The last category was abolished in 1980 and in 1980 the number of abortions came down to 14 703. However, in 1982, the number of legal abortions was 16 839, 1775 for age; 6632 for forbidden relations; 2626, danger to the embryo; and 5796, danger to the woman. Clearly the last category has been used by the abortion committees as a substitute for the category which was abolished.

9. During July–August 1987 the debate on the desirability of the transfer of the Palestinians out of Israel and the occupied territories held major newspapers' headlines in Israel. This happened when central figures in the Israeli establishment (to differentiate from supposedly marginal rightists like Rabbi Kahana), like ex-General Rekhavam Zeevi and the Undersecretary of the Ministry of Security, Michael Dekel, spoke publicly in defence of the idea, and moreover presented themselves as mere followers in that respect of the major pre-1948 labour zionist leaders, like Berl Kazenelson and David Ben-Gurion.

10. The average number of children of Jewish women in Israel in 1984 was

2.7, while it was less than two, if not one, in most Western countries. For systematic comparison of the situation of women and the family in Israel and in other countries, see Y. Peres and R. Katz, *Megamot*, 26.1, 30–43 (Hebrew).

11.   I myself am an 'historical product' of Ben-Gurion's call for 'Internal Aliya' (immigration) in the early 1940s when the news of the Nazi Holocaust started to arrive. . .

BIBLIOGRAPHY

Azaryahu, S. (1977) *The Organization of Hebrew Women for Equal Rights in the Land of Israel* (Hebrew) (Keren Leezrat Haisha).

Bailin, Y. (1985) *The Price of Unification: the Israeli Labour Party until the Yom-Kipur War* (Hebrew) (Revivim).

Beveridge, W. (1942) *Report on Social Insurance and Allied Services* (London: HMSO).

Davis, U. (1987) *Israel: Apartheid State* (London: Zed Books).

Demographic Centre (1979) *Goals and Means of Demographic Policy* (Hebrew) (Labour and Welfare Ministry).

Edholm, F. O. Harris & K. Young (1977) 'Conceptualizing Women', *Critique of Anthropology*, vol. 3, no. 9, 101–30.

Ehrlich, A. (1980) 'Zionism, Demography and Women's Work', *Khamsin* no. 7, 87–106.

Ehrlich, A. (1983) 'The Oriental Support for Begin – a Critique of Farjun', *Khamsin*, no. 10, 40–6.

Farjun, E. (1983) 'Pax Hebraica', *Khamsin*, no. 10, 29–39.

Ghilan, Maxim (1974) *How Israel Lost its Soul* (Harmondsworth: Penguin).

Halevi, I. (1986) *History of the Jews* (London: Zed Books).

Harris, O. & M. Strivens (1981?) 'Women and Social Reproduction', unpublished paper.

Hazleton, L. (1978) *Israeli Women – the Reality behind the Myth* (Hebrew) (Idanim).

Hecht, D. & N. Yuval-Davis (1978) 'Ideology without Revolution: Jewish Women in Israel', *Khamsin*, no. 6, 97–117.

Kahane, M. (1983) *Thorns in Your Eyes* (Hebrew) (Jerusalem, Institute of Jewish Ideas).

Land, H. (1978) 'Sex Role Stereotyping in the Social Security and Income Tax System'. in J. Chetwynd & O. Hartnett, *Sex Role Systems* (London: Routledge & Kegan Paul).

Leon, A. (1970) *The Jewish Question, a Marxist Interpretation* (Pathfinder Press).

Lehrman, D. (1987) 'Feminism in Israel – a Common Struggle?', *Khamsin* 13, 94–8.

McIntosh, M. (1981) 'Gender and Economics', in K. Young, C. Wolkowitz & R. McCullugh (eds) *Of Marriage and the Market* (London: CSE Books).

Orr, A. (1983) *The Unjewish Staff* (Ithaca Press).

Peres, Y. & R. Katz, 'Family and Familiality in Israel' (Hebrew) *Megamot*, vol. 26, no. 1.

Prime Minister's Committee (1974) *Report on Children and Youth in Distress* (Hebrew).

Ronen, H. (1982) 'Israeli Arabs Multiply Faster than the Chinese', *Bamakhane* (army weekly; Hebrew), 17 November.

Shahak, I. (1981) 'The Jewish Religion and its Attitude to Non-Jews', *Khamsin* nos. 8 & 9, 27–61 & 3–49.

Shamgar, L. (1979) 'War Widows in Israeli Society, (Hebrew), Ph.D thesis, Hebrew University.

Sharit, A. (1985) 'Is Israel Withdrawing from the Army?' (Hebrew), *Koteret Rashit*, 15 May.

Smooha, S. (1978) *Israel – Pluralism and Conflict* (London: Routledge & Kegan Paul).

Svirsky, S. & D. Bernstein (1980) 'Who Worked in What, for Whom and for What' (Hebrew), *Booklets for Research and Critique*, no. 4, 5–66.

Wilson, E. (1977) *Women and the Welfare State* (London: Tavistock).

Yishai, Y. (1978) 'Abortion in Israel – Social Demand and Political Responses', *Policy Studies Journal*, vol. 7., no. 2 (Winter)

Yuval-Davis, N. (1982) *Israel Women and Men: Divisions Behind the Unity* (Change Publications).

Yuval-Davis, N. (1984) 'The Current Crisis in Israel', *Capital and Class*, no. 22 (Spring) 5–14.

Yuval-Davis, N. (1985) 'Front and Rear: the Sexual Division of Labour in the Israeli Army', *Feminist Studies*, vol. 11, no. 3 (Autumn) 649–76.

Yuval-Davis, N. (1987) 'Marxism and the Jewish Question', *History Workshop Journal*, no. 24 (October) 82–110.

7 Women and Reproduction in Iran
Haleh Afshar

INTRODUCTION – IRAN: STATE AND NATION

With the rise of fundamentalism and the imposition of its values on the daily lives of Iranians, women are firmly directed towards domesticity and selected as the bastions of honour and familial respectability. The family is seen as the centre and motherhood as the nexus of nationhood. The imposition of motherhood as the sole national obligation of Iranian women has been exacerbated by the long-running war against Iraq. The reproduction of future martyrs has become the patriotic duty as well as the function of womanhood. This chapter examines the political context within which this has occurred alongside an examination of women's position in contemporary Iran.

Iran is a land of diverse tribal and regional people with one religion; 99 per cent of Iranians are Muslims and of these almost 90 per cent are Shi'ias. But though united in religion, Iranians are widely divided in their ethnic origins, cultural backgrounds and social practices. Persian, which is now recognised as the national language, is merely the language of the largest minority which has, through state control of the educational system and the media, been imposed as the *lingua franca*. The process of unification of the nation through explicit state policies dates from the modernisation policies of Reza Shah Pahlavi in the 1920s.

The secularisation process was part and parcel of Reza Shah's attempt to modernise Iran within a very short period of time. He saw two major obstacles to this process: the religious establishment, which remained the bastion of traditional and 'backward' ideology; and tribes who presented a major threat to the emerging centralised national government. All the major tribal groups were defeated within the first decade of the Pahlavi's rule (1921–78). To ensure their continuing subjugation, Reza Shah placed all the major tribal chieftans, *Kavanin*, under house arrest in the capital Tehran. Subsequently, both Reza Shah and his son Mohamad Reza Shah married daughters of tribal chieftans to forge a political alliance with these groups and secure their allegiance. The *Kavanin* made the best of the situation by acting as intermediaries between the regime and their people, and seeking to represent the interest of the minorities in the capital. In the long run, the children of many of these chieftains grew up in the city and went abroad to be educated. They returned home as town dwellers, and found it difficult, if not impossible, to return to the rigours of nomadic life. At the same time, Reza Shah sought to force tribal people to abandon their migratory lifestyle and settle in selected villages, although this policy was only partially successful and at times exacerbated tribal feuds.

There are deep divisions among tribal groups and regions. Tribal groups, who are ethnically of different origins, stretch across national boundaries. The Kurds live in Turkey, Iran and Iraq, and the Baluch in Pakistan as well as Baluchestan. Similarly, the Arab Khamsin tribes in the south are closely related to their Arab relatives across the river Shat'al Arab. But tribal allegiances did not and do not imply unity; the Kurds are divided among themselves and, as the Iraquis observed, the Khamsins in Khuzestan were not willing to support their Arab brethren in their invasion of Iran.

The central policy authority in Iran has traditionally relied on inter- and intra-tribal differences to maintain its control. The policy continued during the Pahlavi era and the divisions between ethnicity, tribalism and nationhood played an important role in permitting the establishment of a relatively secure and secular centralised government. Nevertheless, tribalism continues to provide both a strong sense of identity and a basis for struggle against the encroachment of state policies in the country.

THE STATE AND THE RELIGIOUS ESTABLISHMENT

The religious establishment has traditionally provided an alternative arena for the struggles against the state. Shi'ias do not recognise a secular head of state empowered to exercise political control over the nation. The only legitimate ruler, according to the Shi'ia, is the Imam, the direct male descendent of the prophet. The Iranian constitution of 1906 asserted that the nation's religion is the Isthna Asahri Shi'ia Islam, and endorsed much of the Islamic dictum, particularly where the domestic sphere was concerned. Accordingly men were recognised as the legal head of the household and enabled

to exercise considerable power over their wives and children including the unequivocal rights of divorce and custody of children.

Although the religious establishment retained a critical view of the
state, it shared the bureaucracy's distrust of minorities and denied the
validity of the many regional and local varieties of interpretations
that Islam has had in Iran. Religious beliefs can become diluted in
different regions and have frequently been influenced by local
superstitions, saints and sufis. These local cults can easily be accom-
modated by the flexibility of Islamic ideology. But the religious
establishment has always resisted such fragmentation of its central
authority and the *ulama* have usually supported policies that imposed
and maintained a sense of national unity. This is surprising since, in
essence, nationhood is a relatively unimportant concept in Islam. The
whole Muslim community, *Ummat*, is seen as one people guided by
total submission to the rule of Islam which, by its nature, transcends
national and international boundaries.

Despite its conservative nature, the Iranian religious establishment
has spearheaded many revolutions and uprisings in Iran's recent
history. In the first instance, these were to protect traditional
interests as a whole and the merchant classes in particular against the
penetration of foreign interests in the country. There is a close
alliance between the bazaar, the commercial and financial centre of
the merchant economy, and the *ulama*. The Shah's decision to
welcome foreign capital immediately alienated both the church and
the merchants. Nevertheless, by the turn of the century the Shah
continued to hand out commercial monopolies to foreign capital.
Iranian banking, customs and excise, oil and even the gendarmerie
were handed over to foreign control at a rapid pace. The bazaar and
the *ulama* reacted by staging a revolution and calling for a con-
stitional monarchy. The ensuing constitution in 1906 appointed a
group of *ulama* to supervise all future legislations with the right to
veto over those that contravened Islamic dictum.

The constitution did not recognise any of the national minorities
and Farsi was declared as the *lingua franca*. The *ulama*, who aspired
to *umma* and its concepts of universality, saw the emergence of a
centralised Muslim state as a useful step towards a utopia of Muslim
unity. Tribal and ethnic divisions, as well as differences in languages
and religious interpretations were, in turn, viewed as potential
threats to such an ideal state.

With the arrival of the Pahlavis, the *ulama* began losing much of
their control over the social and political life of the country. They had

been the main source of education, carried out exclusively for boys, and main source of legal decisions, running the *shariat* ('religious') courts and controlled all registries, public endowments and private trusts (Keddie 1961–2). Reza Shah instituted secular education and judiciary systems. He imposed secular taxes, which undermined *khoms*, and set up an extensive and secular bureaucracy, gradually eroding much of the power of the clergy, and curtailing their lucrative source of income.

The secularisation process was to prove of great benefit to women, who began to gain access to education and the formal labour market.

WOMEN AND SECULARISATION

The Iranian constitution of 1906 barely recognised women as legally independent individuals. Despite their important contribution to the revolution, they were not given the vote and were legally defined as dependent wives and daughters within male-headed households. It took Iranian women nearly 30 years to gain equal access to education and another 30 to get the vote. Men's arbitrary rights of polygamy and divorce took yet another decade.

Reza Shah's modernisation policies, however, proved invaluable to the liberation of women. In 1937, Reza Shah issued a decree for compulsory unveiling. Iranian women were officially barred from wearing the all-enveloping *chador* and required to appear in public dressed in Western-style clothes. Iranian men were also encouraged to wear Western-style clothes, as were civil servants. The ban on the veil was preceded in 1936 by the simultaneous admission of male and female students to the newly inaugurated University of Tehran. Women, in their capacity as mothers, were viewed as crucial links in the modernisation process, and an effective means of transmitting the secular ideology to the new generations.

Nevertheless, the civil code, enacted in 1932, did not radically change the social and legal position of women. The law closely followed the Islamic Sharia laws, the only deviation was the raising of the age of marriage to 15 for girls and 18 for boys.

By contrast the criminal code, enacted in 1940, was modelled on the *code Napoléon* and its formulation closely followed the Belgian model. It was a final blow to the *ulama*'s legal authority and abandoned much of the Islamic practices, such as equating the word of one male witness with that of two females, or banning women from practising the law. Nevertheless, the code accorded men the right to murder their adulterous wives, mothers or sisters without giving similar rights to women.

WOMEN, MARRIAGE AND THE WOMEN'S MOVEMENT

The Shah's liberating measures provided an opening for the women's movement to continue its struggle for emancipation and equal rights particularly in the domestic sphere. Within the family women in general and wives in particular were accepted as socially subordinate and unequal, and had little legal recourse against husbands. Polygamy was legal: four permanent and numerous temporary marriages, *siqeh*, which could be for as short or as long a period as the husband wished. Men had the legal and unilateral right to divorce and custody of children (boys at four and girls at seven years), without any right of access for mothers. It was the man who decided where the family should live, and whether the wife was permitted to work or travel abroad; in both cases women had to obtain formal permission granted in the presence of a public notary. Ironically, although a wife's identity was clearly defined in terms of her husband, women were not legally permitted to change their surname to that of their spouse on marriage.

Marriage was a formal means of granting control over women, their sexuality, their fecundity and their daily lives to the husband. Women retained their Islamic right to their personal wealth and property and the inalienable right of inheritance. But their husband could so circumscribe their lives as to make these material rights irrelevant.

All Iranian women were unavoidably subject to the marriage laws, since it was illegal for them to marry foreigners without the formal permission of the Ministry of the Interior. Foreigners who married Iranian women were required either to become Muslims or to suffer imprisonment for infringing the law. Curiously enough, it was the foreign husband and not the woman who was so punished. Iranian men, however, were not subject to such restrictions; they could marry anyone they wished at any time and any place. But, since civil marriages were not recognised by the state, all those who married Muslim men had to convert to Islam. The father bestowed his name, nationality and religion on the children and thus it was legally impossible for Muslims to have legitimate non-Muslim children.

The women's movement gained some impetus from the secularisation policies and spent the period 1940 to 1962 in formulating and fighting for its demands. The major issues were the vote, direct and equal access to the labour market and curbs on the extensive domestic control by husbands. The early 1960s were years of political turbulence which included massive street demonstrations and strikes, organised by middle class and professional women. Finally in 1963 women got the vote. Once enfranchised middle class women made rapid strides in the public sphere, by 1978 there were 38 women judges, one woman minister, five deputy ministers, one ambassadress and 400 university lecturers.

By the 1970s the arena of the women's struggles had shifted to the domestic sphere. Already in the mid-1960s the institution of marriage was showing signs of weakness in Iran. The country had the fourth-highest rate of divorce in the world and one in every four marriages resulted in separation. In all these cases women lost the custody of their children and had little other than their *mahre*, a sum negotiated and recorded in the marriage contract which is payable to the bride for the consummation of the marriage. Normally this is received by wives on divorce rather than at the time of marriage. Given that husbands could prevent their wives from working and stipulated where and how they lived, divorced women often found themselves unemployed, in a strange city, with few friends or relatives and no visible means of livelihood.

The 1967 and 1975 Family Protection Laws finally curbed polygamy and men's unilateral right of divorce. The Family Law Courts were interposed between men and their Islamic rights of marriage and divorce. The first wife's consent was required before a second marriage was permitted and custody was made subject to the court's decision, and women who gained custody were entitled to claim alimony. The husband's right to decide on a wife's occupation was tempered by a similar right on the part of wives; for the first time ever Iranian women seemed poised on the brink of legal equality.

The Shah, whose personal opinions of women were quite unacceptable, chose to support their case for a number of reasons. In the context of the rapidly modernising economy women provided a plentiful and cheap source of labour and could be used to displace the more troublesome men in many of the processes of production. To do so women had to be relatively free to choose their employment. As to the middle class women, they were an obvious and vociferous support base for the Shah who, particularly in the early 1960s, had little popularity.

The land reforms which began in 1962 alienated the wealthy landed gentry and the religious institution who controlled much endowed and shrine lands. Similarly, the merchants who used land holdings as secure investment were vehemently opposed to these measures. At the same time, the Shah's decision to close the *Majlis* ('Parliament') and rule by decree alienated many of the middle classes and severely undermined his legitimacy as a ruler. Without the support of the army, the monarchy would not have survived the decade. As it was, rebellions, strikes and demonstrations were the order of the day. In this context the support of women was seen as a valuable political asset. Furthermore, the central role that women played in the socialisation of future generations was seen as an obvious means of gaining the backing of future generations for the rule of the Shah. His influential twin sister, Ashraf Pahlavi, was appointed as head of the Women's Organisations and the way was paved for radical legal reforms.

Not all women, however, supported the feminists. In particular the insistence on sexual freedom and the rejection of marriage, family and the traditional notions of shame, modesty and dignity alienated the majority of Iranian women. For the impoverished working class women the provisions of the Family Protection Laws were largely irrelevant. They did not know about them and had no means of securing those rights. Access to the formal labour market was, however, a welcome opportunity with their domestic duties. Furthermore, it was frequently the husband and father of employed women who negotiated and obtained their wages. Thus the economic boom of the 1960s did not necessarily benefit the working class women.

Some middle class women were also weary of feminism. The more traditional mothers feared the disregard for family honour exhibited by their daughters. Often mothers of feminists resorted to marrying off their younger daughters straight from school to prevent them from embarking on the immoral venues of liberation. As to the majority of Iranian men, they saw the liberalisation process both as a direct threat to their position of social and economic superiority and as a rapid erosion of their familial status. Not surprisingly the Islamic backlash found extensive support.

Once more the clergy spearheaded a revolution in 1978. The anti-American and anti-imperialist rhetorics were backed by constant references to the national loss of honour and dignity. This usually meant the loss of control over sexuality and reproductive activities of women, and a resulting loss of face and national identity. Women as well as men supported the claims that the country as a whole was losing its moral standards. The religious backlash offered among other things the reinstatement of the natural social order and the affirmation of family as the core and motherhood as the nexus of nationhood.

It would be all too easy to dismiss these views as anti-feminist and retrograde, but since the mass of Iranian women did and still do share these views it is essential to analyse why they emerged, why they found such a wide acceptance and why they continue to attract an inordinately large number of women.

It is crucial in this context to understand the emotive and cultural importance of concepts such as honour and dignity. Muslim women in general and Iranians in particular did and still do accept the burden of respectability. In Iran as in many other Third World countries, family honour is defined in terms of the sexuality of women and the ability of men to control and exchange women and their reproductive powers. Women themselves share these views which attribute disgrace to those who choose to deviate from the norm. It is those women who have deeply imbibed the male ideologies who are now instrumental in both maintaining and transmitting these traditional standards.

Marriage is central to the transfer of control over reproduction and the marriage market, which is largely organised and run by women. Mothers are instrumental in choosing prospective marriage partners and assessing their wealth, health and suitability. Thus, although men negotiate the actual marriage contract, women control the future of their children. Not surprisingly mothers see the process as desirable and empowering and a means of becoming something of a matriarch within the domestic sphere. So long as the traditional values are maintained all mothers have the prospect of power and prestige. Once the married couple produce children, then grandmothers are accorded the prestige of the custodians of family health, welfare and morality. Traditional ceremonies run by women and for women initiate and protect each and every stage of child-rearing and enhance the authority of older women over the family as a whole. Even working class women whose wages support the husband and numerous children see motherhood as an essential part of their life and cherish the prospect of retiring into grandmotherhood. For them children are the only available source of financial security at old age and grandchildren a means of gaining familial control and authority.

To deny the aspirations of the majority of women towards self-fulfilment through motherhood would in practice mean the denial of an active support base for any 'feminist' movement in Iran today.

To see marriage and motherhood as oppressive institutions imposed by men to control women is correct in terms of the theoretical analysis. But it is irrelevant in terms of tactics and strategy in a country where the majority of women lamented the liberation of their daughters because it resulted in the denial of marriage and blocked the natural progress towards maternal control of the domestic sphere. This resistance was not confined to the lower and lower middle class women; it was as much an intra-class division as an inter-class one.

Women in Iran, as women elsewhere, were faced with a widely segregated labour market, where few had any hope of gaining a secure livelihood through their waged employment and where all continued to carry out their domestic obligations. It is therefore hard to see any firm grounds for them to support what they saw as degrading materialistic policies which denied their importance as mothers, yet gave them little power and opportunity to succeed outside the marital framework. Repressive as they are, the current Iranian policies of domestication of women create a clear and important role that many women appreciate and value; motherhood is now a national duty and publicly revered.

MOTHERHOOD AS A NATIONAL DUTY

In adopting motherhood as a national duty, the current regime is endorsing the views of the more traditionalist women, as well as appealing to those who did not find life under the Pahlavis particularly liberating. Most women were all too aware of their marginality to the oil boom and the ensuing bonanza. But now they have been given a central role to play, a role which they have always had but have never been applauded for by the entire state propaganda machine. The new regime is cleverly equating domesticity and motherhood with being 'pivotal in securing the continuation of Islam and its values'.[1] Women are told they are crucial because they 'raise brave men in their laps' (Khomeini, *Kayhan*, 17 May 1980). This 'natural' function ensures the very survival of the system. Khomeini, the 'great leader of the revolution' categorically confirms this view: 'so long as you ladies play your part and raise our youths, this Islam will go forward' (*Kayhan*, 14 March 1985).

The expansionist aims of this 'forward' movement are for the moment absorbed at the Iraqi borders. The Iranian government, however, has no intention of ending this war which has taken the lives of thousands of youths. What is required of women now is to play their 'decisive part' in this encounter and 'raise good children for the battle fronts' (*Kayhan*, 30 November 1986), to protect Islam and 'achieve all the ambitions of humanity' (Khomeini, *Kayhan*, 17 May 1980). Motherhood has become a public duty as well as an heroic one. 'You heroic women of Iran, you carry hope and wisdom on your back and the future generations in your hands. It is you who must bring the cargo of revolution to a safe harbour'.[2]

It is by returning to the heart of the family that Iranian women have become 'central', 'pivotal', 'invaluable' etc, attributes that were not commonly given to the 'weaker sex' in the pre-revolutionary days. The family is offering salvation to all woman-kind and saving them from the horrors of feminism and society from total destruction:

> Women in some western countries have strayed from the natural limits of their unborn selves and gone beyond the social and natural requirement. This has brought suffering and destruction to the women themselves and to society as a whole.
>
> As a result of such inappropriate behaviour in the west, in the name of women's liberation, whole generations of children are left uncared for and unprotected. They have become like soulless, mechanical beings devoid of human sensitivities.[3]

It must be noted that in the context of the current public discourse in Iran, 'the family' is meant to be interpreted as motherhood: 'In truth only a wise, caring and religious mother can raise an ideal child, no man has the capability of fulfilling such a role. This is a characteristic ability that nature has bestowed on women.'[4] The synonymous use of *family* and *motherhood* is so prevalent that male orators never think of mentioning fatherhood as a necessary part of 'the family'. Men, Iranian women are told, 'have to carry the heavy burden of heading the household and it falls upon them to manage its complicated financial transactions'.[5] It is not easy for those middle class women who fought for equality throughout the century to accept defeat. Yet many women have come to see motherhood as an achievement as well as a national duty.

MOTHERS AND MARTYRDOM

The question of feminism and inequalities may have had a very
different impact had there been no war. But the Iranian revolution
has for but one of its eight years of existence been at war. This war
has used men as gun fodder. The entire nation is mobilised and males
of all ages, as young as 12 or as old as 65 are encouraged to come
forward and give their lives for the cause. An atmosphere of hysteria
is nurtured by the media, the religious establishment and the
government, and all are promised a gateway to heaven through the
saintly road of martyrdom. Martyrdom, however, is the sole domain
of men. It is one of the 'separate and special rights reserved for men
in Islam'.[6] Women are merely the mothers, wives or sisters of
martyrs. In this atmosphere of heightened hysteria, women have
become the guardians of cradles and coffins (Afshar 1982). Mothers
of martyrs attend Friday prayers, address the gathered multitudes
and talk of the 'blood-stained shrouds' of heroes. Some announce
that they have given as many as five sons to the revolution and will
have more on offer (*Kayhan*, 5 October 1985).

Newspapers report the sweet sorrows of mothering martyrs:

> The messengers of hope and pride, they were at the graveside of
> the martyrs. The place which enshrines our hopes and sorrows and
> those of thousands, no tens of thousands of scarlet oaths of love;
> the place which is the centre of hope for smitten mothers and which
> exerts a calming influence on all.
>
> Mothers of martyrs, their wives, sisters, children and their
> relatives all visit the graves on pilgrimage to celebrate the new
> year. Under their salt tears they smile in the knowledge of the
> eternal happiness, seeing the soldiers fulfilling their engagement to
> shed their blood and march triumphantly towards eternal spring.
> (*Kayhan*, 29 March 1987)

It is as mothers that women have created both the youths and their
bravery:

> This love and commitment which has sprung among our youth is
> rooted in the sacred tears that fall from the eyes of the mothers of
> martyrs at the feet of our martyred imam Hosein. The tears
> entwined with the milk that the suckling babies drink at the
> fountain of their mother's breast. What a unique mana and reward.
> This mixture of tears and milk imbibed while hearing about the

heroic deeds of the martyrs of Islam, this is the spiritual food that raises our devout martyrs. (*Kayhan*, 17 March 1985)

Mothers are encouraged to follow the examples set by those who gave their sons to the cause of Shi'ism, a sect born of blood and martyrdom. Mohamad's son in law Ali sought to follow the prophet and become the caliph of Muslims. In the event he failed to do so and finally took up arms against the sunni caliph. It was an unequal struggle and Ali and many of his male descendants died in some of the bloodiest of battles. Iranians have revered all these imams, and their heroic deaths are the themes of stories repeated regularly; particularly during the month of Muharam when these battles occurred. Men and women have traditionally gathered to hear of these heroic deeds, and cry for their saints. The imagery of tear-stained suckling babies does reflect the reality of the experience of many of the less wealthy classes. It has always been assumed that crying for the imams paved the way to heaven for the believing shi'ias.

Since the revolution this oral tradition has been taken on board by the newspapers who frequently print similar tales. One that is obviously addressed to women was published in the popular daily newspaper, *Kayhan*:

Vahab ibn Abdolah ibn Habab Kali was one of the followers of martyred imam Hosein. His mother said unto him 'rise my son and help the descendant of the Prophet.' He responded 'Rest assured that I would not fail in this duty.' He went forth and killed many a foe and returned. 'Oh mother, are you pleased with the deeds of your son?' His mother responded 'I will be totally satisfied only when I see that while leading the men of imam Hosein, May God Hail his Soul, you are killed in battle.' (17 March 1985)

An anonymous young woman writing to *Kayhan* exhalts the ability of women to cope with suffering and reminds her sisters of Omeh Leila:

Be like the wife of Imam Hosein Omeh Leila who watched while the enemy cut the throat of her husband, then her son and all her children before her very eyes. The heartless enemy killed them in that desert of Kerbala without even giving them a drop of water to quench their saintly thirst. (15 May 1985)

Such obviously bloodthirsty language is not viewed as obscene by the readers. In fact, it is thought to reflect the powerful poetry and the graphic experience of suffering for a just cause.

The language of death and joy are intertwined. Martyrs announce in their last letters home: 'I chose to espouse the gun and share my life with the holy war *jehad*, May God bless this union.'[7]

But, whereas martyrs may marry death, women and particularly war widows are expected to remarry fast and continue to reproduce: 'Widows of martyrs must not be hidebound by archaic traditions of sorrow and mourning, they must gather their offspring and move on to a new husband.'[8] Since women have been squeezed out of the public sector, those who lose their breadwinners become an instant problem. Despite many statements of intent, the government has nothing, other than glory, to bestow on wives of martyrs. They have been officially classified as 'the unprotected', and in 1983 the Majlis passed a bill instructing the government to 'submit, within a three months period, the necessary legislation and appropriate budget for protection of the unprotected women and children'.[9] But although by 1987 the government was spending an annual average of 15 billion rials on the children of the martyrs and war casualties (*Kayhan*, 19 April 1987), their wives remain 'unprotected' and continue to be viewed as a social 'problem'.

Even worse is the 'problem' of single girls. The speaker of Majlis Hojaloleslam Hahsemi Rafsanjani has publicly denounced the terrible phenomenon of 'unmarried women' as 'Western-style urban depravity'. At a Friday prayer meeting he lamented the fact that:

almost one in every seven women has no husband . . . What can we do with them? The society must think about this problem. We have 4 to 5 per cent more men than women and the number of unmarried men is also greater than that of women . . . Obviously the Islamic solution is to encourage these women to get married. The Majlis must try and introduce measures to secure this process. We must think about this one-seventh of our female population and think how we would feel if we were so deprived. (*Kayhan*, 2 November 1985)

Naturally, the unmarried men are not seen as a 'deprived' and 'problematic' lot, they are destined to 'espouse' martyrdom. Now the pressure is on women to marry disabled war returnees or embark on temporary or polygamous marriages. 'Honour', 'grace' and 'pivotal' roles are all the preserve of mothers, all other women, particularly the unmarried ones, are merely 'problems' that can only be solved by marriage and reproduction.

The new regime embodies the ideological backlash against feminism. All the legal ground gained in the past 70 years was repealed within the first seven months of the Islamic rule. Men have regained their right to polygamy, though in the case of permanent marriages this is made subject to the approval of Family Courts. Permission is granted to all men who are deemed able to support more than one wife and to all who wish to marry war widows regardless of their economic means. Temporary marriages are not subject to any control nor to any maximum numbers. Men are entitled to have an unlimited number of concubines who, like permanent wives, must 'obey' their husbands and never deny them their sexual demands. Men can also divorce at will. Temporary wives have no recourse to the law, permanent wives may go to court to claim their *mahre*. Fathers and paternal ancestors have legal custody of all children and their consent is needed by a spinster who wishes to marry.

Not only have men gained total control of the domestic sphere, but also women are now required to become socially invisible by adopting the Iranian *chador*, a garment that covers them from top to toe, or a similar Islamic *hejab* ('veil'). Those who refuse to do so are subject to 79 lashes, which are administered immediately. Nurseries have been closed down as 'dens of subversion' and mothers of young children are not permitted to work full-time. Although officially women are not barred from seeking employment, with the exception of teaching and nursing, they are finding it ever more difficult to obtain jobs.

CONCLUSION

The problems of living in an Islamic society, aggravated by the soaring prices of food and accommodation and the cuts in civil service salaries have made it impossible for many women to espouse the idealistic views of Islamic domestication. The struggles of daily life, the ever-longer queues, the ration cards that cannot be exchanged for food, the empty shelves in government shops, shortages of everything for those who have little money and abundance for the wealthy who can pay the exorbitant black market prices, are all contributing to the increasing disillusion among many of the poorest women. But the loss of hope is in many cases tempered by the massive war hysteria and the emphasis placed by the state in its expressed admiration for and endorsement of motherhood. Mothers of past and future martyrs are called upon at every turn to save the nation, its honour and its war against the oppressor. Mothers of martyrs are not only honoured by speeches but also entitled to extra rations, to better resources and to favourable treatment across the board. The combination of expressed honour and actual economic rewards makes it easier for mothers of martyrs to live in the hope of seeing the Islamic utopia which has a special place for such mothers. Motherhood has become a personal aspiration for unmarried women who are forever encouraged to embark on the 'sacred duty of motherhood' as soon as it is physically possible. The family is hailed as the saviour of the future of the nation and the women are the instruments chosen by God and the country to secure this future. Women have become part and parcel of the mechanisms for producing and educating 'martyrs'. As educators of martyrs they are deemed to be in full-time employment and in need of neither formal education nor paid employment outside the home. Girls' schools are increasingly concentrating on a segregated curriculum training women to become good mothers of martyrs and the few university places that are available are strictly segregated. Women are not admitted to scientific and engineering subjects and even agriculture and rural development has been defined as unsuitable for women. This, in a country where women are the sole cultivators of the staple food, rice.

The clergy and the media continue to exalt the 'natural' sensitivity of women and their 'natural' reluctance to embark on any intellectual pursuit quite unsuited to their tender psyche. They have become designated as unequal before the law, they are unable to give evidence unsupported by a male witness and are in many cases entitled to half as much justice as their male counterpart (Afshar 1985). All this because of the assumption that women have no place in the public and formal sector and require no protection in the private domestic one.

The inherent contradictions of this world view of domesticity and the real need of most mothers to work in order to pay the exorbitant rents, the ever-rising prices is proving a more effective means of raising women's consciousness than the polemics of feminists' arguments presented by middle class women. The situation is exacerbated now that the bombs are falling on cities and attacking homes in the capital city, for there is nowhere to go and little protection. The government is of the view that self-reliance is needed if the country is to survive. Self-reliance is proving more and more to be reliance on women to secure the survival of the family. But for most women, although the expectations are emphatic, there are few legal means of achieving this end. The contradictions between the ideology of domestic bliss and the reality of survival through the war is becoming too extreme. The war hysteria is increasingly tempered by demands for a peaceful settlement and many women find themselves supporting the call for peace since they are less and less able to fulfil their heroic role of warmongers.

NOTES

1. Hojatoleslam Hosein Mirkhani, Director of the Political Ideology Unit of the Tobacco Co., *Kayhan*, 22 June 1986.
2. Maryam Behrouzi, MP for Tehran, speaking in the Majlis (parliament).
3. Hojatoleslam Hashemi Rafsanjani, Majlis Speaker, *Kayhan*, 26 July 1984.
4. Ibid.
5. Ibid.
6. Hojatoleslam Movahedi Kermani, MP and member of Islamic Propaganda Unit, *Kayhan*, 2 March 1986.
7. Martyr Naser Farrajalahi, *Kayhan*, 8 October 1981.
8. Ayatolah Mohamadi Guilani, member of the Council of Guardians.
9. Law for the Protection of Unprotected Women and Children.

BIBLIOGRAPHY

Keddie, N. (1961–2) 'Religion and Irreligion in the Early Iranian Nationalism', *Comparative Studies in Society and History*, vol IV, 289.

Afshar, H. (1982) 'Khomeini's Teachings and their Implications for Iranian Women', in *In the Shadow of Islam* (London: Zed Press) 27–75; and *Feminist Review*, no. 12 (October) 59–72.

Afshar, H. (1985) 'The Legal, Social and Political Position of Women in Iran', *International Journal of the Sociology of Law*, no. 13, 47–60.

8 Women and the Turkish State: Political Actors or Symbolic Pawns?

Deniz Kandiyoti

In 1987 Turkey was a country offering the perplexing spectacle of a sit-in and hunger strike by ultra-religious women students demanding the right to don the veil to go to classes (a right officially denied), and a small group of feminists marching through the streets to demonstrate against violence against women, virtually in the same week. While to an outside observer this may seem merely a healthy manifestation of political pluralism, the roots of the contemporary situation have to be sought in the specificities of the woman question in Turkey and of its evolution through time.

The role played by the Turkish state after the establishment by Mustafa Kemal Ataturk of a secular republic in 1923 on the remnants of the Ottoman Empire, has represented nothing short of an all-out onslaught on existing social institutions and mores surrounding the status of women. It is little wonder therefore to find that most discussions of the woman question in Turkey tend to centre around the republican legal reforms, their meaning and possible strategic importance for the state. These reforms were extensive. The Turkish Civil Code adopted in 1926, inspired by the Swiss Civil Code, outlawed polygamy, gave equal rights of divorce to both partners, and granted child custody rights to both parents. Women's enfranchisement followed in two steps: women were first granted the vote at local elections in 1930 and at the national level in 1934. These rights were not obtained through the sustained activities of women's movements, as in the case of Western suffragist movements, but were granted by an enlightened governing elite committed to the goals of modernisation and 'Westernisation'. It is a fact that the reforms remained merely formal for a long time especially in the rural areas most weakly integrated into the national company, and class-biased in that they primarily benefited the women of the urban bourgeoisie. Nonetheless, their very existence signalled a new positioning of the state *vis-à-vis* the woman question which deserved to be explained.

First-generation republican women writers tended to stress the intrinsic necessity of these reforms in the development of a democratic, civic society (Taskiran 1973; A. Inan 1964). More recently, Tekeli has suggested that women's rights have played a strategic role both against the political and ideological basis of the Ottoman state and with respect to establishing proofs of 'democratisation' *vis-à-vis* the West. She argues that singling out women as the group most visibly oppressed by religion, through practices such as veiling, seclusion and polygamy, was central to Ataturk's onslaught on the theological Ottoman state which culminated in the abolition of the caliphate in 1924. The timing of the legislation on women's suffrage in the 1930s, on the other hand, is interpreted as an important attempt on the part of Ataturk to dissociate himself from the European dictatorships of the time (nazi Germany and fascist Italy) and claim Turkey's rightful place among Western democratic nations (S. Tekely 1981).

While this intepretation concurs well with analyses of the strategic role of women's rights in other revolutionary situations (Massell 1974; Molyneux 1981: 167–202), an exclusive emphasis on the finalities of the republican reforms may unwittingly obscure the historical developments which led up to them. The aim of this chapter is to demonstrate that the 'woman question' has been central to the different ideological and political reactions to the dissolution of the Ottoman empire in the latter half of the nineteenth century and the beginning of this century. Since the eighteenth century the Ottoman Empire was increasingly unable to hold its own either against Western economic/military supremacy or against the rise of nationalist, secessionist movements in its provinces. This weakening of imperial power ushered in a period of political search and redefinition which lasted until the First World War and culminated in the Kemalist republic in 1923 (Berkes 1964; Shaw & Shaw 1977; Lewis 1961; Timur 1968). It is particularly over this period that the 'crisis' of Ottoman culture and of the Ottoman family system appeared on the political agenda. As a result, women made an irreversible entry into political discourse and the question of their rights became a privileged site for debates concerning questions of modernisation vs. cultural conservatism and integrity. In what follows, I will attempt to trace the development and transformations of the woman question during the period leading up to the Republic in order to highlight how the treatment of this question closely paralleled successive shifts within the Ottoman/Turkish policy and reflected its changing political priorities.

The drive for Ottoman 'modernisation' is officially traced to the Tanzimat period (1839–76), despite earlier attempts at technical innovation in the military sphere. By the time of the Second Constitutional Period in 1908, the relative merits of the Islamist, Ottomanist and Turkish solutions to the impasse of the Ottoman state had become a matter of public debate. It is important to emphasise that the various, overwhelmingly male, protagonists of the woman question also represented distinct ideological positions on a way out of the floundering empire. The dilemma posed by Westernisation and the need for progress on the one hand and the maintenance of Ottoman culture and integrity on the other strongly coloured the debate on the status of women and infused the general polemic with high levels of emotionality.

The Islamists saw the reasons for decay in the corruption and abandonment of Islamic law and institutions and advocated a return to the unadulterated application of the Sharia. Their political solution revolved around a pan-Islamic empire consolidated around the institution of the caliphate. Although the adoption of Western technology was deemed acceptable in the military and economic spheres, Western culture must on no account be allowed to contaminate the values of Islam. Not surprisingly, the position of women came to represent the touchstone of such contamination and any attempts to discuss issues such as polygamy, veiling and unilateral male repudiation in divorce could be denounced as morally corrupt or irreligious.[1] This contrasted sharply with the views of the Westernists, who maintained that the superiority of the West resided not only in its technology but in its rationalistic, positivistic outlook, freed from the shackles of obscurantism and stifling superstition. To varying degrees, they held Islam responsible both for obscurantism and for what they saw as the debased position of women (which some went as far as pinpointing as the major symptom of Ottoman backwardness (Mardin 1962). The Ottomanists ever since the Tanzimat reforms had been trying to formulate a balance between Westernism and traditionalism by achieving an 'Ottoman' synthesis (Mardin 1962).

Loyalty neither to Islam (actively mobilised during the reign of Abdulhamit II, 1876–1909) nor to the Ottoman cause would prove effective. By the turn of the century an Anatolian-based, predominantly Turkish nation was becoming an established fact. The current of Turkism which lay the foundations of Kemalist nationalism played a key ideological role in ensuring the transition from an empire based on the multi-ethnic *millet* system to a nation–state. It is within this current that we see the principal stirrings of feminism in Turkey which have left their mark on all subsequent treatments of the woman question. The specific form and content of the discussion on women's emancipation under Ataturk's republic is thus directly traceable to the birth and development of Turkish nationalism. This point will be illustrated with particular reference to Ziya Gokalp who is considered as the main ideologue of Turkism and who has put forward a clear and detailed position on the woman question. This chapter will explore the key moments in the transformation of the woman question in the Ottoman Empire leading to the birth of Turkish nationalism, culminating in the era of Kemalist reforms. The implications of this analysis for an understanding of the contemporary situation will be spelt out in the conclusion.

THE TANZIMAT REFORMS AND THEIR AFTERMATH

The decline of the Ottomans signalled by two centuries of military defeat and territorial retreat called for more radical reforms than earlier attempts at modernisation which had been confined to the adoption of Western military technology, training and organisation. The Tanzimat period set the scene for extensive reforms in the fields of administration, legislation and education. They were instrumental in the rise of a new class of Ottoman bureaucrats, relatively secure in their position within a secularised bureaucratic hierarchy, and weakened the overall political influence of the clergy (*ulema* as well as their monopoly over the educational system. These reforms have been the subject of conflicting intepretations, denounced by some as total capitulation to the West and assessed by others as the foundation of all later developments in the creation of a secular state. It seems beyond doubt that the Ottoman Empire suffered serious peripheralisation *vis-à-vis* European powers since the sixteenth century, so that the Tanzimat reforms can be seen as being primarily aimed at creating a central bureaucracy which could become an instrument of the smooth integration of the Ottoman state into the world economy (H. Inan 1983: 9–39). Already the trend of capitalising on Ottoman military misadventures to wrest trade concessions and force the lifting of tariff barriers was well established.[2] Indeed, the official document that ushered in the Tanzimat, the *Gulhane Hatt-i Humayunu* ('Imperial Rescript of Gulhane') had as its net effect the extension of legal assurances to non-Muslim and non-Turkish mercantile groups affiliated to European commercial interests. The new role that the Tanzimat bureaucracy had to adopt meant that it had to articulate itself to the needs of what they saw as 'modernisation' and to the expectations of Western powers in a manner that alienated the groups and classes which were excluded from the new 'modernised' structures (such as craftsmen, artisans, the urban lower middle class, petty civil servants and not least the ulema) and in fact stood to lose from them. These classes were to become the focus of a resistance which often took Islamic forms. Thus the Tanzimat reforms were to create deep cleavages in Ottoman society which were reflected both at the institutional level and that of culture more generally.

An interesting case in point is the dual legal system which emerged in a series of attempts at both renovation and compromise. Despite the importation of numerous European laws in the Tanzimat period as well as Abdulhamit II's autocratic rule, the personal status code affecting women directly had been untouched by new legislation. The preparation of the Ottoman Civic Code by a commission headed by Cevdet Pasha represented a compromise, by attempting a modern Ottoman code based on the Sharia. However, a religious opposition headed by the Sheyh-ul-Islam subsequently persuaded Abdulhamit to disband the commission which had only completed the legislation concerning debts and contracts, thereby blocking any further changes in the fields of family and inheritance laws. This created a dual juridical system whereby secular courts (*mahkeme-i nizamiye*) functioned under the aegis of the Ministry of Justice, while religious courts (*mahkeme-i ser'iyye*) remained under the jurisdiction of the Sheyh-ul-Islam. Nonetheless, the Tanzimat introduced some modest legislative advances concerning women with the promulgation of the 1856 Land Law (*arazi Kanunu*) granting equal rights of inheritance to daughters and the ratification of a treaty abolishing slavery and concubinage. Similarly there were some innovations in the field of women's education. However, Taskiran (1973), in her review of these advances, comments on the pressures resulting from the strict segregation of the sexes. For instance, she mentions the fact that due to the scarcity of trained female teachers all courses except needlework had to be taught by elderly male teachers.

The Tanzimat period did not necessarily stand out as a period of substantial change in matters regarding women but rather as a period of intellectual ferment when ideas about Ottoman society, the family and the position of women started to be debated in a variety of fora and media, from the newspaper column to the novel. The cultural cleavages between a Western-looking bureaucratic elite and popular classes committed to and protected by Ottoman communitarian conservatism were reflected in key literary productions of the time in which the Westernisation of upper class males and the position of women in society represented privileged and recurrent themes. Mardin's (1974) analysis of the post-Tanzimat novel suggests that whereas such as Ahmed Mithat Efendi echoed the popular unease with Westernisation through satirical treatment of the superficial, Western-struck male, there was a discernible consensus among the elite with regard to women's emancipation which was discussed in universalistic 'civilisational' terms. This, however, was an issue which apparently had the potential to create important cleavages among men of different social extraction. To the lower classes, any change in the position of women had been and remained anathema and a sign of moral decay. Nor was the elite necessarily consistent: retrenchment into conservatism *vis-à-vis* women always remained just below the surface. For instance, as late as 1917, and at a juncture when the Empire was in grave peril, the Committee for Union and Progress halted all progressive leanings and constituted a committee to discuss the suitable length for women's skirts. Enver Pasa removed one of his commanders in the Dardanelles whose daughters he had seen sunning themselves on the Bosphorus (Rifki Atay 1974: 433–4). This and similar observations lead Seni to conclude that the divisions between the traditionalists and modernists may have been more apparent than real:

> If the modernists distinguish themselves from the conservative current in terms of the real measures adopted for the emancipation of women, they do not escape the moralism and puritanism of their opponents. It would seem that the control of women also cristallizes a part of their Ottoman identity since when they feel that identity, the Ottoman Empire, to be under threat they backtrack in their position and regress to more conservative attitudes. (Seni 1984: 89)

There is thus a clear continuity, in her view, between the imperial edicts of the sixteenth century making women's attire and movements the object of direct legislation and later more modernist interventions on women's behalf, including Kemalist reforms: they all emanate from an Ottoman state tradition that recognises no sources of legitimacy outside itself.

While it is easy to concur that women's bodies have been and are still today used as vehicles for the symbolic representation of political intent, it is more difficult to overlook or dismiss the very real transformations that Ottoman society underwent in the transition to the republic and their independent impact on the position of women. Nor do these transformations stand in any mechanical or easily understandable relationship to the woman question. On the contrary, the attempts to absorb new positions into existing views of the world or ideologies often created complex, convoluted bodies of discourse.

There is little doubt that the Tanzimat elite was deeply influenced by the ideals of the French Enlightenment and that some of this influence was reflected in writings on the position of women. Not surprisingly, however, that most strenuous efforts of early feminists were directed towards making their demands compatible with the dictates of Islam. Even Fatma Aliye Hanim, the most noteworthy woman writer of her time who distinguished herself through a lively polemic on polygamy with the conservative Mahmut Esat Efendi, clearly inscribed herself within such a perspective. Nor was it an accident that the longest-lived woman's weekly of the time, *The Ladies' Gazette*, declared itself to be serving three principles: being a good mother, a good wife and a good Muslim.

In contrast to the nationalist stance of later periods, Islam was the only available body of discourse in which the woman question could be debated. Ozankaya's discussion of the work of Semseddin Sami, one of the most enlightened Tanzimat thinkers, illustrates the limitations of even the best-meaning attempts at tackling the woman question (Ozankaya 1985). Sami is ultimately unable to openly criticise Islamic rules regarding divorce, polygamy and wife-beating even though one can quite easily sense his unease with them throughout his text, titled *Women*. Universal human rights, rationalism and positivism notwithstanding, even the most progressive proposals regarding women had a strong instrumentalist flavour about them. Traditional marriages and repudiation were denounced as the source of 'social ills' weakening and corroding the social fabric, the ignorance of women meant that they were lacking as educators and mothers and finally the gulf between the sexes created by the traditional family system was a source of alienation and unhappiness for both. Yet I disagree with contention that these concerns represented an emulation of Western, particularly Victorian ideals of monogamy and female domesticity by a rising bourgeois ruling class (S. Tekeli 1982: 179). I think there are specific and very significant reasons for the fact that men were the most outspoken critics of the Ottoman family system and, on occasion, the most fervent advocates of romantic love or at least marriages based on mutual compatability.[3] The traditional Ottoman family, based on deference to the *pater familias* and seniority, arranged marriages and spatial and social segregation of the sexes was not conducive to rapport and closeness between spouses, much less to romantic love. It should not suprise us that it was 'modern' men who could openly reflect upon the oppressiveness of traditional family structure although women were more visibly the victims of it. Women, on the other hand, may have been more timid or at least cautious in this respect. It is revealing that the author Omer Seyfettin accuses women themselves of standing in the way of more companionate relations between the sexes (Seyfettin 1926, 1963). This is hardly surprising in a society which offered women no shelter outside the traditional family and a tenuous one inside it; where the options, however undesirable, of spinsterhood, 'genteel' female occupations and female religious orders were totally unavailable. Duben (1985: 117) also notes the high rate of remarriage among widows in contrast to the Mediterranean and Russian patterns of the time, so that at no stage were women visible as the managers of their own property. At least initially, women may have had a great deal to lose and very little tangible gain in following the steps of their more emancipated brothers. The 'passive' attitude of women on this issue was to last well into the republic and continue to draw fire from progressive men.

THE SECOND CONSTITUTIONAL PERIOD: THE SEARCH FOR A NATIONAL BOURGEOISIE

Beneath Tanzimat liberalism were powerful undercurrents which had a strong material basis. The Tanzimat reforms had failed to stem the tide of nationalism in the Christian Balkan provinces and had essentially strengthened the hand of local Christian merchants who were the preferred trading partners of European powers in Ottoman lands. In Berkes' terms, the more Westernisation proceeded, the more Turks felt excluded from it (Berkes 1965). After an abortive attempt at constitutional monarchy (1876–8), followed by an Islamist backlash under the rule of Abdulhamit II, the Second Constitutional

Period was ushered in by the Young Turk's Revolution. The Committee for Union and Progress, who were the architects of the 1908 revolution, did not delay in seeing that the Ottoman nationalism which united Muslim and non-Muslim subjects in the overthrow of Abdulhamit's despotic rule in a bid for 'freedom' could not stem the secessionist movements in the ethnically heterogeneous provinces. Toprak suggests that Turkish nationalism, which was born from the liberal currents of the 1908 revolution, also represented a reaction against liberalism, especially against economic liberalism which had cost the Muslim artisan so dear.

> The nationalism which the Second Constitutional Period put on the agenda, aided by the extraordinary circumstances of World War I, produced a yearning for the creation of a Muslim–Turkish 'middle class', which after the loss of the war was to constitute the cadres of the National Struggle in Anatolia. (Z. Toprak 1982: 21)

The search for alternatives to liberalism produced a major shift in thinking about society and economy in the direction of corporatism which in the case of the Second Constitutional Period represented a blend of solidarism emanating from French corporatist thought and Ottoman guild traditions (Z. Toprak 1980: 41–49). Throughout the war years the Committee for Union and Progress (CUP) consistently struggled to create a middle class consisting of Turkish–Muslim entrepreneurs, stressing the ethnic dimension of the problem persistently and favouring Muslim over non-Muslim. The effects of this national mobilisation on women have not received the attention they deserve except in connection to the war effort, a point to which we shall return later. It seems probable, however, that women were not totally unaffected by the new societal priorities. A suggestive though inconclusive example may be found in the effects of a law imposing Turkish as the language of correspondence to foreign firms operating in the Ottoman Empire in 1916. These firms had previously employed foreigners and now had the choice of either folding up or recruiting local employees. Meanwhile, vocational evening classes especially in the fields of commerce and banking were instituted by CUP clubs, in an obvious attempt to create skilled cadres that were competent in these fields. Special business classes for women were also started. Especially at a juncture where male labour was getting scarcer because of the war, the Advanced School for Commerce had opened a section for women in the Women's University (*Inas Darulfununu*) which was so popular that a second section had to be opened

(Z. Toprak 1980: 83). Undoubtedly this type of vocational training must have been instrumental in creating new employment opportunities for women. However, the real social upheaval that propelled women into the workforce in greater numbers was the First World War itself.

THE EFFECT OF THE WARS

The overthrow of Abdulhamit's absolutist rule and the greater freedom promised by the 1908 revolution raised hopes among women that they would also benefit from the new principles of liberty and equality. However, these hopes soon turned to disillusionment and bitterness. A woman's periodical, on the occasion of the fifth anniversary of the Constitution proclaimed that it was 'men's National Celebration Day' (Taskiran 1973: 38). Nonetheless, the Second Constitutional Period saw an increase in the numbers of women availing themelves of education opportunities, increases in the number of women's associations and periodicals and especially a tendency for women themselves to participate more actively in the women's struggle. Many writers on this question put these developments down to the effect of the wars on women's greater involvement in public life (S. Tekeli 1982: 198; Abadan-Unat 1981: 8).

Already during the Balkan War middle class women were involved in social welfare activities. The women's branch of the Red Crescent had started training Turkish nurses. However, it is during the First World War that the massive loss of male labour to the front created a demand for female labour, not unlike the case of the other warring nations. The growth of female employment did not remain confined to white collar jobs but involved attempts at wider mobilisation thoughout the Anatolian provinces. A law passed in 1915 by the Ottoman Ministry of Trade instituted a form of mandatory employment which rapidly swelled the number of women workers. Women volunteers were organised into workers' platoons to help the army with support services. In the agrarian sector, the Fourth Army formed Women Workers' Brigades. The Islamic Association for the Employment of Ottoman Women, founded in 1916, was instrumental in employing women workers under conditions insuring them an 'honest' living. But if the war effort created interest in women as workers there was no less interest in an intensification of their role as mothers and reproducers of the nation. It is interesting and significant

that the Empire's first pro-natalist policies also had the employees of
the Islamic Association for the Employment of Ottoman Women as
their target, for whom mandatory marriage by the age of 21 for
women and 25 for men was introduced. The Association used
newspaper columns for matchmaking, provided girls with a trousseau
and staged well appointed wedding ceremonies. Those who passed
the marriage age limit or did not accept the matrimonial candidates
proposed by the Association had 15 per cent of their salary withheld
and were excluded from membership. Conversely, marriage was
rewarded by a 20 per cent salary increase and similar increases for the
birth of each child (Z. Toprak 1982: 317–18, 412). Thus women's
service to the nation as workers and breeders was made explicitly
co-extensive. Nonetheless, concession had to be made to the necessi-
ties of female employment: in 1915, for instance, an imperial decree
allowed the discarding of the veil during office hours. It is clear,
however, that this increased female presence in the labour force was
viewed with considerable ambivalence. The conditions of women's
work tended to scrupulously respect the segregation of the sexes.
They were apparently often forced by the police to return home if
their skirts were shorter than the officially prescribed length (Yener
1955: 8). There is little doubt that this period must have been full of
confusion and contradictions, leading to mildly comical incidents. In
September 1917 the following announcement was posted on Istanbul
walls by the police:

> In the last few months shameful fashions are being seen in the
> streets of the Capital. All Muslim women are called upon to
> lengthen their skirts, refrain from wearing corsets and wear a thick
> *charshaf*. A maximum of two days is allowed to abide by the orders
> of this proclamation.

This announcement was the subject of such indignation and furore
that higher level administrators were forced to rebuke their overzea-
lous subordinates and retract the order. The new announcement read
as follows:

> The General Directorate regrets that old and retrograde women
> were able to induce a subaltern employee to publicize an
> announcement ordering Muslim women to go back to old fashions.
> We announce that the previous orders are null and void. (J. Melia
> 1929: 147–8)

Clearly, despite women's entry into the workforce in unprecedented numbers and strenuous advocacy for their rights, changes in mores were slow to come. Meanwhile the intelligentsia continued to bemoan enforced segregation and the impossibility of civilised communication between the sexes. The rights demanded by feminists of the time (voiced in publications such as *Mahasin*, which started appearing in 1908; *Women*, again published in 1908 in Salonica; and Women's World from 1913) were relatively modest by later standards. They were the right to education, to go out in the streets and to places of entertainment and a limited right to work with freedom from police harassment. Greater equality within the conjugal union was a largely taboo subject despite the ongoing polemic on the evils of polygamy. Women themselves felt compelled to defend monogamous and more companionate marriages in the name of 'social hygiene' rather than on grounds of greater equality and basic human rights.[4]

The compromises apparent in the 1917 Family Code are quite indicative of the different pressures at work in Ottoman society. This law aimed at completing the task left unfinished by the *Mecelle* (the Ottoman Civic Code referred to previously) by legislating aspects of personal status which had been totally abandoned to the rulings of religious authorities. It was the first written family code in the Muslim world. The contractual aspect of the marriage was to apply to all religious groups in the Empire, it being understood that this could be followed by the appropriate religious ceremonies. Marriages without consent were decreed illegal and divorce was made more difficult by the introduction of a conciliation procedure. However, not only was polygamy not abolished but it was actually legalised even though its practice was made more difficult by stipulating the consent of the first wife. Interestingly, the commission headed by the Minister of Justice, Seyyit Bey, wavered on the question of polygamy and finally accepted it not only in view of the clear Koranic licence in this respect but also on demographic grounds, since numerous wars had created an imbalance in the sex ratio. Needless to say, such a law failed to satisfy either those who wanted to see fundamental changes in the family system considered to be 'in crisis' or those who saw the changes as clear-cut infractions of Koranic law. Minorities were also discontented with what they saw as a curtailment of the authority of their own religious authorities and in 1919 complained to the forces then occupying Istanbul and obtained a repeal of the clauses regarding Christian marriages. This law nonetheless remained in force until 1926 in Turkey and much later in the Ottoman periphery (until 1953 in Syria and Jordan, for instance). It represents an interesting exercise illustrative of the muddled attempts of Ottoman legislators to introduce progressive change. These attempts were to encounter great opposition and resistance throughout this period and extend to Kemal Ataturk's own National Assemblies regardless of women's often praised contributions to the War of National Liberation.

WOMEN AND THE STRUGGLE FOR NATIONAL INDEPENDENCE

The end of the First World War brought about the dismemberment of the defeated Empire and the control of Anatolian provinces by occupying Western powers. The landing of Greek forces in Izmir in May 1919 and the occupation of Istanbul by the British unleashed a wave of popular protest in which women were not merely participants but public speakers in open-air meetings, where they made impassioned calls for the defence of the motherland (Taskiran 1973: 68–73). Many women joined Mustafa Kemal's forces of resistance in Anatolia. Associations for Patriotic Defence started springing up in the Anatolian provinces. Women did not join these directly but set up their own parallel organisations. The Anatolian Women's Association for Patriotic Defence was founded in Sivas in November 1919. The active members were the wives, daughters and sisters of local provincial notables and higher level state employees as well as some teachers and educational administrators. In other words, these were the women of the nascent local middle class which the Second Constitutional Period did so much to nurture. During the War of National Liberation there was a large-scale mobilisation of the whole nation in which Anatolian peasant women played a key and visible role glorified in public monuments as well as patriotic literature. Yet the coalition of nationalist forces which united behind Mustafa Kemal included men of religion who were going to remain inflexible on the woman question to the last and constitute a focus of active and vocal resistance throughout the first and second National Assemblies. In fact in 1924, soon after the declaration of the republic there were some regressive steps in legislation in the field of civil law (Berkes 1973: 68–73). Some of the advantages gained through the 1917 code by endorsing polygyny were endangered by a draft law eliminating the need for consent by the first wife and lowering the legal marriage

age for girls to nine years old. This proposal, which was subsequently rejected, was part of the playing out of the opposition between religious and Kemalist forces in the National Assemblies, an opposition which was finally resolved by the abolition of the caliphate and the abrogation of the Sharia. There is no doubt that the woman question became one of the pawns in the Kemalist struggle to dismantle the theocratic remnants of the Ottoman state (Taskiran 1973: 106–9). Some progressive men were using newspaper columns to take women to task over their acquiescent posture in this debate. Necmettin Sadak wrote thus in the daily newspaper *Aksam*:

> Finally an important issue concerning Turkish womanhood has arisen. The National Assembly has started debating the Family Law proposal. This proposal . . . has passed through the Sharia and Justice commissions without a murmur from women. Almost all newspapers have cried out against this law. However, our women who engage in demonstration with or without justification and at every possible occasion, did not act. We have witnessed this silence with surprise as well as some despair. Where were our young ladies filling sections of university classes, where those founding political parties in the pursuit of chimera? The Turkish Republic is insulting you with its own laws, why are you not crying out? (21 January 1924).

The process of mobilisation and co-operation of women into the ideological struggles of the republic can thus be seen to be significantly different from early feminist movements in the West. In this latter, the women's struggles took place against a background where legislation was lagging considerably behind the socio-economic realities of advancing industrialism and a growing labour movement. In Turkey, it was an ideological lever operating on a substantially unchanged economic base, at least as far as women's economic and familial options were concerned. Yet the specific forms that feminist discourse took continued to be indicative of the search for a new legitimacy in the transition to the republic. From this perspective, the transformations of the woman question can be better understood with reference to republican state ideology than to any other single factor. The main legitimising discourse for the woman question in Turkey has been that of Turkish nationalism, which has its roots in the Turkism of the Second Constitutional Period.

TURKISH NATIONALISM: A NEW FRAMEWORK FOR THE
WOMAN QUESTION?

The woman question remained for a long time caught in the dilemma
between Westernism and Islam without a third term to moderate the
debate. The Turkish movement represented an attempt at recuper-
ation of a national identity which could be grounded in a national
'culture' rather than solely in Islam. This was in many ways a most
difficult enterprise.

As Berkes (Berkes 1965: 52–3) points out, the Turks were the
last to achieve a sense of nationality in the whole Ottoman
formation. In the Ottoman context, Turkish nationalism could
even be perceived as divisive in a situation where other ethnic
minorities were restive, and it certainly found no favour among the
Islamists for whom the notion of a Turkish nation constituted a
threat to the Islamic *umma* (collectivity of believers). Turkish
nationalism initially took the form of a populist reaction to Westernism not unlike, and certainly heavily influenced by, the Narod-
nik movement in Russia and the Turkish Russian emigrés. The
leading ideologue in this transition has undoubtedly been Ziya
Gokalp (1876–1924), the author of *The Principles of Turkism*.
Parla suggests that 'Gokalp's system fixed the parameters within
which mainstream political discourse and action has been conducted in Turkey' (Parla 1985: 7). This is also true of his influence on
the treatment of the woman question throughout the period of
republican reforms. Gokalp, who was greatly influenced by Durk-
heim's sociology, substituted his notion of society with that of
'nation', emphasising the national–cultural rather than Islamic
sources of morality. His work represents strenuous attempts at
defining the nature of the collectivity called 'nation'. He settles on
the idea of a collectivity based on common language and culture
and representing the highest form of social solidarity. Gokalp took
great pains to distinguish the concepts of culture and civilisation
from one another. In his view Islamic and Western civilisation
influences need not be incompatible with Turkish national culture,
although admittedly his brand of Islam, ethical Sufism, is highly
secular, and his preferred Western sources are drawn from European corporatism. Gokalp's search for authentic national–cultural
patterns led him to an eclectic examination of myth, legend,
archeological and anthropological evidence on pre-islamic Turkic
patterns. In his *Principles of Turkism* he spells out the program-

matic implications of Turkism and its application to the fields of language, aesthetics, morality, law, religion, economy and philosophy. His views on 'moral Turkism' especially on family and sexual morality represent a significant departure from earlier approaches to the woman question. He suggested that family morality based on old Turkish cultural values included norms such as communal property in land, democracy in the 'parental' family as opposed to the autocracy of the patriarchal family, the equality of men and women and monogamy in marriage. He traces some of the origins of what he labels as 'Turkish feminism' (using these exact words) to the fact that Shamanistic religion and rituals were based on the sacred power vested in women. This made men and women ritualistically equal, an equality which was seen to permeate every sphere of life including the political. The patrilineal and matrilineal principles were equally important, children belonged to both parents, women could control their own independent property and, interestingly, were excellent warriors ('amazons', to use Gokalp's own terminology). This amounted to a pre-Islamic 'golden age' for women which was made much of by subsequent feminist women writers. As far as Gokalp was concerned the Turks had lost their old morality: 'The reason why Turkists are both populist and feminist is not simply because these ideals are valued in this century; the fact that democracy and feminism were the two main principles of ancient Turkish life is a major factor in this respect' (Gokalp 1978: 148).

This position was not greeted with a total lack of scepticism. Mehmet Izzet, for instance, suggested that Gokalp's ideas might have been greatly influenced by pragmatic considerations: 'At a time when Islamic law was being abolished, when improvements in women's position were sought and changes in family life along the Western model were being introduced, interpreting this movement as a return to ancient Turkish law and national identity would ensure greater goodwill and sympathy' (Eroz 1977: 13). Berkes (1982: 114) also comments rather wryly on the fact that by some happy coincidence the elements of Turkish culture which Gokalp took such pains to distinguish from Western civilisations matched this latter with uncanny ease. Indeed, in terms of the position of women what might have been rather unpalatable in the form of Western influence gained a new legitimacy when it was recuperated by national discourse.

For Ataturk, who was to distance himself from Islam much further than Gokalp himself ever envisaged, the latter's definition of the nation was to provide a very valuable tool. In assessing Kemalist nationalism it is important to remember some of the special circumstances under which Mustafa Kemal's struggle for independence took place. The Istanbul government headed by the sultan-caliph had reached an agreement with the occupying powers to stamp out Kemalist resistance. In April 1920 the Sheyh-ul-Islam issued a *fetva* (canonical proclamation) declaring holy war against the 'Ankara rebels'. A military court condemned Ataturk and a group of his supporters to death and the defection of his forces to the Army of the Caliphate was only reversed after the outrage created by the humiliating treaty of Sevres. Henceforth religious reaction (*irtica*) was to be identified as one of the main enemies of Kemalist nationalism.

Yet unlike Islam, which had very deep roots in the Ottoman–Turkish polity, Turkish nationalism was an ideal which had yet to search for its symbols and discourse. This search, already inaugurated in the work of Turkists and Ziya Gokalp in particular, was to culminate in a major onslaught on Turkish history and an extensive rewriting of it. This task was given to the Association for the Study of Turkish History which was set up by Ataturk himself and which reported its findings to the First Turkish History congress which was held in Istanbul in 1932. This history traced back its origins to Central Asiatic beginnings when the Turkish peoples and the Chinese were the main actors on the scene of civilisation. All the subsequent civilisations of Asia Minor and Mesopotamia were considered as so many links in the chain of Turkish civilisations. Compared to the relatively recent conversion of the Turks to Islam in the tenth century, this history could be traced much further back, to 5000 BC. This was the new framework in which the woman question in Turkey started being discussed by the first generation of Kemalist feminists. The most prominent among these, Afet Inan, who was also Ataturk's adoptive daughter, devotes a long section to a consideration of Turkish women before Islam in her classic book, *The Emancipation of the Turkish Woman* (A. Inan 1962) where she echoes Gokalp's convictions about women's high status and greater equality in pre-Islamic times.

This type of discourse is prevalent among many Third World feminists, but the actual content of it changes according to what it is that is being recuperated by the discourse that claims to be feminists.[5] In the Turkish case, it was nothing less than national identity itself which was deemed to have a practically built-in sexual egalitarianist component. Even though the actual realities of entrenched Ottoman–Turkish patriarchy[6] and the influence of Islam made such pronouncements seem rather remote and endowed them with a mythical quality, they continued to be part of the official discourse on women in Turkey. This meant, furthermore, that an alternative model for Turkish womanhood could be proposed and discussed.

I have suggested elsewhere (Kandiyoti 1988) that the writer Halide Edip Adivar, herself a fighter for the nationalistic cause, played a major role in creating images of the new Turkish woman. Her nationalist heroine is cast as a self-sacrificing 'comrade-woman' who shares in the struggles of her male peers. She is depicted as an asexual sister-in-arms whose public activities never cast any doubt on her virtue and chastity. This echoes the position of Ziya Gokalp who, in his attempt to establish a new nationalist morality in which the equality of women could be justified as an integral part of Turkish cultural mores, nonetheless took great pains to emphasise in his section of 'sexual mores' that the principal characteristic of the Turkish woman was her *iffet*, i.e. chastity and honour. Thus, there appears to be one persistent concern which finally unites nationalist and Islamist discourses on women in Turkey: the necessity to establish that the behaviour and position of women, however defined, are congruent with the 'true' identity of the collectivity and constitute no threat to it. It is perhaps not surprising that the prime area of potential threat centres around women's appropriate sexual conduct and its control, so that the dread of loss of control and anxieties about degeneracy and corruption easily get displaced onto a third term, 'Westernism', which becomes a highly charged, polyvalent symbol.

CONCLUSION

In this chapter, I have attempted to show how the woman question in Turkey became part of an ideological terrain upon which concerns about the changing nature of the Ottoman order and the question of Ottoman and later Turkish national identity were articulated and debated. I have argued that the mobilisation of Turkish women and their co-optation into the political struggles around the dissolution of the Empire and the birth of the republic served as an ideological lever and that the single most important factor accounting for the transformations of the woman question could be found in nationalist state ideology.[7] I have not addressed the material conditions of different classes of women in Turkey, nor their transformations under the impact of socio-economic changes (see Kandiyoti 1977, 1982, 1983, 1984), but instead focused on the crucial role of state ideology. I have alluded quite consistently throughout the text to the possible connection between the demands of the national economy (as in the need for female labour during the First World War), processes of class formation (as in attempting to understand the alliance of forces behind the Kemalist movement) and social practices and ideologies relating to women. However, I have left the link between socio-economic transformations and ideologies relative to women as totally indeterminate and problematic, allowing for the possibility that ideology may be used to both reflect and negate, promote and compensate for such transformations. I would like to conclude by drawing out both the continuing relevance of my analysis to an understanding of more contemporary developments, and the ways in which it needs to be expanded and modified.

At a superficial level, current debates on women continue to express the tensions between Westernisation, Islam and Turkism, and one cannot help but note the persistence of both the concerns expressed and the imagery used to express them. The issues of women's dress and conduct are still used by the state to signify political intent,[8] although women nowadays increasingly appear as active participants and militants in causes concerning them. Yet it would be quite misleading to interpret this semblance of continuity as an extension of past ideological debates playing themselves out within an essentially unmodified state tradition. Although the terms and symbols of the debate may seem thoroughly familiar, it must be acknowledged that they operate in a totally transformed national and international context. Thus any further analysis of the woman question in contemporary Turkey would have to take fuller and more explicit account of changing economic realities and class alignments, the struggles between rival ideologies within the Turkish political spectrum, and their degree of representation at the level of the Turkish state.

Since the First Republic, Turkey has undergone several drastic reorientations in its domestic economic policies and in its mode of insertion into the world economy, with important consequences for the country's class structure, as well as the nature of the Turkish state apparatus (I. Tekeli *et al.* 1984). The fact that Kemalist republicanism (and its cultural Westernism) is no longer the sole ideology emanating from the centre, and that a new political elite with a strong religious orientation, its own cadres and political organisation now exists has been the subject of much recent commentary (B. Toprak 1978, 1981; Saribay 1985). The implications of these transformations for different classes of women in Turkey are as yet hard to ascertain beyond being able to assert that the issue of their roles and place will remain an actively contested domain. The 1970s witnessed a resurgence of polemical writing on women which was more diversified than ever before, since it involved the 'Marxist' left and growing Islamist currents alongside a previously dominant Kemalist position and a proliferation of women's organisations operating as extensions to political parties and movements (Yorgun 1985: 78–83). This has meant that the new protagonists of the woman question became more self-consciously politicised and better organised. It has also meant, however, that just as in the past women have only been able to operate in co-opted political structures, defining their own demands as marginal or secondary to what each tendency saw as their 'main' struggle, i.e. the fight against 'backwardness', imperialism or class struggle, as the case may be. Interestingly, only Islamist currents accord a central place to the position of women, at least at the level of discourse, since they see keeping women in their religiously sanc-tioned traditional roles as absolutely crucial to the maintenance of the Islamic social order. At a time when the tensions between political authoritarianism and democratic pluralism are openly on the Turkish political agenda, it will be interesting to see whether women's movements and feminist currents are able to finally emerge as an added voice in the search for democratisation, or whether women's concerns will continue to be played out in a manner that reduces them to being symbolic pawns. While my incursions into the woman question between the Tanzimat period and the republic do not provide any answers to these contemporary questions, they hopefully suggest a method to begin tackling them.

NOTES

1.   In this connection Caporal draw attention to the fact, unlike the Arab Middle East and Muslim Russia where vigorous modernist Islamic currents could be seen, Ottoman Islam has remained more consistently conservative. B. Caporal, *Kemalizmde ve Kemalizm Sonrasinda Turk Kadini* (Ankara: Turkiye Is Bankasi Kultur Yayinlari, 1982) 736.

2. For instance, Mahmut II's attempts to consolidate Ottoman central authority over the provinces brought him into conflict with Mehmet Ali the powerful governor of Egypt, who he was finally able to subjugate with Britain's naval and military support. The price for such support was the commercial treaty of 1838 which opened the vast Ottoman market to British manufacturers by lifting trade restrictions and tariff barriers.

3. There is a vast literature by male writers of the time on the evils of traditional marriages and the unhappiness and alienation resulting from them. For an impassioned defence of romantic love, see Omer Seyfettin *Ask Kalgasi* (Istanbul: Bilgi Yayinevi, 1964). Seyfettin writes: 'Here in our surroundings, the surroundings of the Turks, love is strictly forbidden. It is as forbidden as an infernal machine, a bomb, a box of dynamite.' (p. 52).

4. This in itself is not surprising and the arguments are frequently reminiscent of the earlier Western feminists such as Mary Wollstonecraft in her *Vindication of the Rights of Women* (1792).

5. Witness the attempts of Muslim feminists to recuperate Islam itself by invoking an Islamic 'golden age' for women which possesses many of the positive characteristics attributed to the pre-Islamic Turkish pattern, including women's equality as warriors (for the faith, in this latter case). As examples, see El Saadawi's 'Women and Islam', and Al-Hibri's 'A Study of Islamic Herstory', both in A. Al-Hibri (ed.), *Women and Islam* (Oxford: Pergamon Press, 1982).

6. Anthropological studies show that despite some regional variations in marriage practices, the patrivirilocal household was normative in Turkey. For a review of the evidence, see Duben (1985).

7. The primarily symbolic function of the rights granted to women may be evidenced in their steadily declining representation in parliament since the First Republic, and especially after the transition to a multi-party system. In the three chambers elected between 1935 and 1946 the number of women representatives was 18, 15 and 16 (rising up to 4.5 per cent with 18 deputies), whereas after 1946 women's representation dropped below 1 per cent and there were never more that 11 representatives at any time. This is readily understandable if we think of it as a shift from a single-party system where the appointment of women by an 'enlightened' vanguard, in line with state ideology, is actually possible to a multi-party democracy where patron–client relationships in the male world play a key role in political competition. For an interesting discussion of male patronage and sponsorship of women politicians in Turkey, see Y. Arat 'From the Private to the Political Realm: Women Parliamentarians in Turkey', in F. Ozbay (ed.), *The Study of Women in Turkey: An Anthology* (UNESCO, forthcoming).

8. As recently as 1982, a Minister of Youth and Sports decreed that schoolgirls would not be allowed to wear short-sleeved blouses and shorts as in the past, but tracksuits covering their limbs completely instead. This announcement was followed by outcries in the more progressive newspapers and satirical cartoons depicting fully veiled

women exercising. Conversely, the growing Islamist current among university youth has been using the official ban on veiling in the classroom as a vehicle for militant protest.

BIBLIOGRAPHY

Abadan-Unat, N. (1981) 'Social Change and Turkish Women', in N. Abadan-Unat (ed.), *Women in Turkish Society* (Leiden: E.J. Brill).

Arat, Y. (forthcoming) 'From the Private to the Political Realm: Women Parliamentarians in Turkey', in F. Ozbay (ed.), *The Study of Women in Turkey: an Anthology* (Paris: UNESCO).

Berkes, N. (1964) *The Development of Secularism in Turkey* (Toronto: McGill University Press).

Berkes, N. (1965) *Baticilik, Ulusculuk ve Toplumsal Devrimler* (Istanbul: Yon Yayinlari).

Berkes, N. (1973) *Turkiyede Caqdaslasma* (Ankara: Bilgi Yayinevi).

Duben, A. (1985) 'Nineteenth and Twentieth Century Ottoman–Turkish Family and Household Structure', in T. Erder (ed.), *Family in Turkish Society* (Ankara: Turkish Social Science Association).

Eroz, M. (1977) *Turk Ailesi* (Istanbul: Milli Egitim Basimevi).

Gokalp, Z. (1978) *Turkculuqun Esaslari* (Istanbul: Inkilap ve Aka Kitabevleri Koll. Sti).

Inan, A. (1962) *The Emancipation of the Turkish Woman* (Paris: UNESCO).

Inan, A. (1964) *Ataturk ve Turk Kadin Haklarinin Kazanilmasi* (Istanbul: Milli Egitim Basimevi).

Inan, A. (1983) 'Osmanli Tarihi ve Dunya Sistemi: Bir Degerlendirme' *Toplum ve Bilim*, vol. 23, 9–38.

Kandiyoti, D. (1977) 'Sex Roles and Social Change: a Comparative Appraisal of Turkey's Women', *Signs*, vol. 3, 57–73.

Kandiyoti, D. (1982) 'Urban Change and Women's Roles: an Overview and Evaluation', in C. Kagitcibasi (ed.), *Sex Roles, Family and Community in Turkey* (Bloomington: Indiana University Turkish Studies), 101–20.

Kandiyoti, D. (1982) 'Economie monétaire et roles des sexes: le cas de la Turquie', *Current Sociology*, vol. 31, 213–28.

Kandiyoti, D. (1984) 'Rural Transformation in Turkey and its Implications for Women's Status', in *Women on the Move: Contemporary Changes in Family and Society* (Paris: UNESCO).

Kandiyoti, D. (1988) 'Women as Metaphor: the Turkish Novel from the Tanzimat to the Repubic', in K. Brown *et al* (eds), *The State, Urban Crisis and Social Movements in the Middle East and North Africa* (Paris: L'Harmattan).

Lewis, B. (1961) *The Emergence of Modern Turkey* (London: Oxford University Press).

Mardin, S. (1962) *The Genesis of Young Ottoman Thought* (Princeton: Princeton University Press).

Mardin, S. (1974) 'Superwesternization in Urban Life in the Ottoman Empire in the Last Quarter of the Nineteenth Century', in P. Benedict and E. Tumertekin (eds), *Turkey: Geographical and Social Perspectives* (Leiden: E.J. Brill).

Massell, G. (1974) *The Surrogate Proletariat: Muslim Women and Revolutionary Strategies in Soviet Central Asia, 1919–1929* (Princeton: Princeton University Press).

Melia, J. (1929) *Mustafa Kemal ou la renovation de la Turquie* (Paris), quoted in B. Caporal, *Kemalizmde ve Kemalizm Sonrasinda Turk Kadini* (Türkiye Iş Bankasi Kultur yayin lani).

Molyneux, M. (1981) 'Women in Socialist Societies: Theory and Practice', in K. Young, C. Wolkowitz & R. McCullagh (eds), *Of Marriage and the Market: Women's Subordination in International Perspective* (London: CSE Books).

Ortayli, I (1983) *Imparatorlugun En Uzun Yuzyili* (Istanbul: Hi Yayin).

Ozankaya, O. (1985) 'Reflections of Semseddin Sami on Women in the Period before the Advent of Secularism', in T. Erder (ed.), *Family in Turkish Society* (Ankara: Turkish Social Science Association).

Parla, T. (1985) *The Social and Political Thought of Ziya Gokalp 1876–1924* (Leiden: E.J. Brill).

Rifki Atay, Falih *Baris Yillari* quoted in Mardin 1974.

Sadak, Necmettin (1924) 'Hanimlarimiz ve Aile Hukuku Kararnamesi' *Aksam* (21 January), quoted in Taskiran 1973.

Saribay, A.Y. (1985) 'Turkiyede Siyasal Modernlesme ve Islam', *Toplum ve Bilim*, vol. 29/30, 45–64.

Seni, N. (1984) 'Ville ottomane et répresentation du corps féminin', *Les Temps Modernes*, no. 456–7 (July–August), 66–95.

Seyfettin, Omer (1926) *Gizli Mabet*, in *En Güzel Hikayeler* (vol. II) (Istanbul: Sander Yayinlari, 1976), 220–8.

Seyfettin, Omer (1963) *Bahar ve Kelebekler*, in *En Güzel Hikayeler* (vol. II) (1976).

Shaw, S.J. & E.K. Shaw (1977) *History of the Ottoman Empire and Modern Turkey*, vol. 2 (Cambridge: Cambridge University Press).

Taskiran, T. (1973) *Comhuriyetin 50. Yilinda Turk Kadin Haklari* (Ankara: Basbakanlik Basimevi).

Tekeli, I. C. Keider, E. Turkcan, G. Yalman, N. Ekzen, O. Purel & K. Boratov (1984) *Turkiyede ve Dunyada Yasanan Ekonomik Bunalim* (Ankara: Yurt Yayinlari).

Tekeli, S. (1981) 'Women in Turkish Politics', in N. Abadan-Unat (ed.), *Women in Turkish Society* (Leiden: E.J. Brill).

Tekeli, S. (1982) *Kadinlar ve Siyasal Toplumsal Hayat* (Istanbul: Birikim Yayinlari).

Timur, T. (1968) *Turk Devrimi: Tarihi Anlami ve Felsefi Temeli* (Ankara: Sevinc Matbaasi).

Toprak, B. (Sayari) (1978) 'Turkiyede Dinin Denetim Islevi', *Siyasal Bilgiler Fakultesi Dergisi*, vol. 1/2.

Toprak, B. (Sayari) (1981) 'Religion and Turkish Women', in N. Abadan-Unat (ed.) *Women in Turkish Society* (London: E.J. Brill).

Toprak, Z. (1980) 'Turkiyede Korporatizmin Dogusu', *Toplum ve Bilim*, vol. 12, 41–9.

Toprak, Z. (1982) *Turkiyede Milli Iktisat (1908–1918)* (Ankara: Yurt Yayinlari).

Yener, E. (1955) 'Eski Ankara Kiyafetleri ve Eski Giyinis Tarzlari', *Dil Tarih ve Cografya Fak. Dergisi*, vol. 13, no. 3, quoted in Abadan-Unat (1981).

Yorgun, P. (1985) 'The Question and Difficulties of Feminism in Turkey', *Khamsin*, vol. 11, 70–85.

9 Women and Nationalism in Cyprus
Floya Anthias

INTRODUCTION

Given the centrality of nationalism in the political history of Cyprus within the last 50 years or so it is not surprising that the issue of nationality should be the one remaining bastion of formal male superiority in the present territorially divided state. The recent Sex Equality legislation (Chappa 1987: 11) has one proviso – the exclusion of regulations concerning nationality from its reform. It remains a male privilege to pass on automatic citizenship to one's children. A woman of Cypriot origin can only do so if she is unmarried and there is no legal father. On the other hand, if she is married to a foreigner she is denied this as an automatic right although as a permanent resident she may apply for her children to be granted nationality.

This chapter analyses some of the ways in which gender relations within the Greek-Cypriot population of Cyprus interlink with ethnic ideology and nationalist practice. As such it does not address the issue in relation to Cyprus as a whole. Cyprus also has a Turkish–Cypriot population which at the present does not accept the legitimacy of the state structure and has declared its own independent state – hence the island is territorially and ethnically divided. However, similarities and differences with the Turkish-Cypriot sector will be noted where possible.[1]

Cyprus is a small island in the eastern Mediterranean which is still defined in international law as one nation–state. It contains within it two ethnic and religious communities which are territorially separated, six armies, a no-man's land, a foreign invader and an illegal second state which purports to represent the Turkish-Cypriot community (Hitchens 1984). There is at the moment of writing a stalemate on the issue of what is to be the resolution to this latest phase of what is called the 'Cyprus problem'. The fate of the 200 000 Greek-Cypriot refugees in the south of the island is still in the balance. The movement of populations along ethnic lines, with the

150

Turkish invasion of Cyprus in 1974, has created territorial separation of the two main ethnic groups on the island for the first time in its long history of foreign invasion and domination. In addition about 60 000 settlers from the Turkish mainland have been imported as part of the demographic 'race' on the island – prior to 1974 only 18 per cent of the population were Turkish-Cypriot. The incorporation of the refugees within what is now effectively the Greek-Cypriot sector in the south of the island has led to a fundamental restructuring of Cypriot society on all fronts. Rapid social change has occurred in the traditional roles and expectations of women, particularly amongst refugee women and younger women in general. Class relations have been complicated by the growth, for the first time, of a landless proletariat, the dispossessed refugees and by the new social division of refugee/non-refugee.

In discourses and policies emanating from the Greek-Cypriot state (when now referring to the state in Cyprus we mean the legitimate state in the Greek-Cypriot sector) women and gender divisions find expression primarily on two levels. First, there is the symbolic level that uses those characteristics ascribed to women to foster the interests of the nation. Symbolism around women's reproductive role and sexual nature are important here. The links between the notions of 'mother' and 'nation' are found almost universally and in many societies special honour is due to the 'mother of the patriot' and Cyprus is no exception here, particularly since national issues and struggles are a central feature of political and social life. At the more practical or policy level many of the concerns of the nation–state have women as a central subject; all those, for example, that are aimed at structuring or restructuring the form of the family which may be instigated by a concern with controlling the mode of reproduction of state subjects in its fullest sense. We can single out as particularly significant all those policies that are aimed at women's reproduction, such as population policies, which in many ethnically divided societies would attempt to maintain or change existing demographic patterns. Rules relating to the conditions under which a legitimate national subject is reproduced are also significant here such as those which may prohibit or provide disincentives to marry outside one's ethnic group. Laws that specify the conditions under which a woman might or might not belong to the national collectivity and have the right to reproduce its subjects, such as nationality laws, are also important.

NATION AND STATE IN CYPRUS

In Cyprus the form of the Cypriot state was externally imposed (Attalides 1979), meeting the needs and desires of neither of the two main ethnic groups on the island – the Greek-Cypriot and the Turkish-Cypriot. Indeed what put insurmountable obstacles to the formation of a common national consciousness within the state structure was its construction via thoroughgoing bi-communalism and separate development for the two groups, with reference to political representation, education and family law, all those processes that can act, where they are common, to cement a nation–state.

Cypriots have never talked about a Cypriot *nation* as such although they have recognised and indeed desired the nation–state structure. The constitution, established in 1960 when Cyprus won its blighted and circumscribed independence, is still valid in international law. One unified nation–state was created, although bi-communalism was written into the constitution at all levels (Kyriakides 1968). Two separate communities were formally designated, the Greek-Cypriot and the Turkish-Cypriot, with their own specified political representation. The Greek-Cypriot community, according to the constitution, comprises all citizens who are of Cypriot origin, have Greek as their mother-tongue or who share the Greek cultural tradition and belong to the Greek Orthodox religion. The Turkish-Cypriot community, on the other hand, comprises all citizens who are of Cypriot origin and have Turkish as their mother-tongue or share the Turkish cultural tradition and are Muslims. The other communities on the island, the Armenians and Maronites, who comprise approximately 3 per cent of the population, can opt to belong to either, although most have opted to belong to the Greek-Cypriot community. However, the issue of who belongs to each community and who belongs to the state is more complicated than might appear from the above legal definitions. For example, non-residents of Cypriot origin – that is, migrants and their descendants – have a formal and automatic right to be included in these communities and the right to residence. They also have automatic right to Cypriot citizenship, which is a requisite for employment in the public sector. Only those who were not resident in Cyprus between 1955 and 1960 for any period cannot hold dual nationality and must forgo their other nationality (e.g. British) if they wish to become Cypriot citizens. In this way, the communities who comprise the state extend beyond the geographical and juridical spheres of the state of Cyprus and are defined by their ethnicity. It is worth noting here that more people of Cypriot origin live outside Cyprus than within its territorial boundaries.

In order to discuss the links between gender divisions and the nation state we need now to give a brief summary of the developments that have led up to the present day.

ETHNIC DIVISIONS

Cyprus has suffered from continuous colonisation because of its strategically favourable geographical position. In 1571 the Ottomans captured Cyprus from the Venetians and introduced what became a Turkish-Cypriot population. Under the Ottoman 'millet' system, which gave internal autonomy to separate religious communities, the Greek-Orthodox Church assumed a position of dominance and became the political and moral representative of the Greek-Cypriot population. Britain was leased the island in 1878 and formally annexed it at the Treaty of Lausanne in 1923. Cyprus finally won its independence in 1960.

The British colonial phase from 1878–1960 gave an impetus to the growth of polarised ethnicities and heralded the growth of ethnic conflict (Coufoudakis 1976). Conflict between Greek-Cypriots and Turkish-Cypriots, however, is a fairly recent phenomenon – the first outbursts dating to only about 30 years ago. Indeed, there is much evidence to show that the two groups lived under what has been termed 'traditional co-existence' (Kitromilides 1977), that solidarity bonds existed between them and that conversions to Islam were fairly common. A common 'Cypriot' dialect incorporated within it a mixture of Greek and Turkish as well as Italian and French.

Although both Muslims and Christians shared the common economic life of rural Cyprus they also had their own separate cultural practices (Attalides 1977). Although they attended each other's festivities, they rarely intermarried. Mixed marriages were not regarded as desirable by the Greek Orthodox Church. For Muslims, on the other hand, mixed marriages were possible between Muslim men and non-Muslim women but not the other way round. Under Ottoman rule there is some evidence that some Christian girls were forced to marry non-Christian men. For example, William Turner (Aimilianides 1938: 32) says: 'They [the Turks] frequently marry the Greek women of the island, as their religion permits a Turkish man to marry an infidel women though to guard against an abandonment of Mahometanism it forbids a Turkish woman to marry an infidel.'

Intermarriage also took place between Christians and the sect of Linobambakoi, who were crypto-Christians, that is were Muslims but spoke and dressed like the Greek-Cypriot population. These had either converted to Islam to avoid the tax that non-Muslims paid or were Latins who were forced to convert to avoid being pursued out of the country (Kitromilides 1977). Most had Christian names and celebrated Christian religious feasts. Until 1889 mixed marriages, like all marriages, were not the concern of civil law but religious law. After 1889, if one of the parties was a British subject this was a case for civil law (excluding Greek-Orthodox and Muslims). In the 1920s mixed marriages had to be by civil law (Aimilianides 1938).

It is not possible in this chapter to give an account of the processes by which the 'passive' ethnicity of the two groups was converted into an active nationalist consciousness and practice. Suffice it to say that the role of British colonial rule was of fundamental importance (Attalides 1979; Anthias & Ayres 1983), as was that of the Greek Orthodox Church. The failure of the socialist movement to harness some of the genuinely anti-colonialist and liberationist tendencies that existed may also be a relevant factor (Anthias & Ayres 1979). All these internal processes, however, have to be seen in the context of the intervention by Western political interests in Cyprus in the war for spheres of influence and the use of Cyprus as a military base for NATO (Hitchens 1984).

Ethnic conflict has its origins in the Greek-Cypriot *Enosis* (union with Greece) movement and the Turkish-Cypriot response, *Taksim* ('partition') (Attalides 1979). Although Cyprus was granted formal independence in 1960 the constitutional arrangements proved unworkable. In 1963 Turkish-Cypriots withdrew from the constitution and into their own enclaves – the physical separation of the two communities saw its beginnings here. In 1974, after a right wing coup staged by the extremist nationalist Greek-Cypriot group EOKA B, under the aegis of the fascist Junta in Greece, Turkey invaded the island, annexing 40 per cent of Cyprus territory in the north of the island. The enormous economic and social changes that have followed cannot be dealt with in this chapter, although those that are particularly relevant for the links between gender, ethnicity and the state will be explored in the following section.

WOMEN AND THE NATION IN CYPRUS

Immediately after 1974 posters appeared everywhere in the south of the island depicting an anguished black-clothed woman, her face tormented and her clothes ragged, and underneath the words 'Our martyred Cyprus'. This representation contained both the symbolism of Cyprus as a woman mourning for her loss and the reality that actual women faced, whose sons and other family had been killed and whose homes were abandoned in the war. This part of the chapter will consider a number of ways in which women relate to national concerns. Firstly, it considers the ways in which sexuality and marriage link to ethnic exclusivity. Secondly, it looks at the role of women within the national liberation struggle. Thirdly, it gives an account of discourses around refugees and the centrality of women within them. Finally, it turns to population policies which are concerned with ensuring the continuing demographic majority for Greek-Cypriots.

Sexuality and marriage

The control of women within the family ensures that women marry within the collective and according to the cultural, legal and religious rules that prescribe what constitutes a 'good Greek Orthodox' woman. The Greek-Cypriot family is nuclear in ideal form, but may include cohabitation by other members of the family, especially widowed parents. Traditionally, there existed an arranged marriage system. Marriages were usually locally based and co-villagers were generally preferred as marriage partners, since their family history was known and they could be trusted.

Great stress was always placed on female sexual purity and 'honour'. Marriage involved the transfer of property through the dowry contract (*proikosymphono*), which was required by the eccle-siastical courts on betrothal. Both parties needed to be Greek Orthodox in order to marry in church. Marriage and family law still remain under the jurisdiction of the ecclesiastical courts. Intermar-riage with the other ethnic groups on the island was extremely rare and for women always entailed the rejection of their own culture and religion, since communal identity was established through the husband.

Marriage arrangements were generally conducted through inter-mediaries who were older married women who were 'in the know' concerning who was available for marriage. They were entrusted with the initial bargaining in relation to the dowry. More recently close relatives or the parents will make the initial approaches, with their children generally having the right of veto in what can be regarded as a collective decision on the part of the family group (St Cassia 1980). As a general rule men move into their wives' locality since it has been common for the woman to bring a dowry house on marriage for the last 50 years or so (Loizou 1976).

The sexual control of women functions to ensure that the males of the group produce their biological descendants and the 'purity' of their 'stock' is assured. In Cyprus until quite recently women were allowed no contacts with men outside the family unit and the family's honour was dependent on female sexual purity. Women could be divorced if they were discovered not to be virgins on their wedding night – a bloodied sheet was displayed as 'proof' of the wife's virginity during the marriage celebrations. Men, on the other hand, were encouraged to find sexual outlets and to prove their 'manhood' – usually through going regularly to prostitutes in the towns.

Women were important in a number of ways as keepers of the cultural rules that controlled women. Firstly, they were the guardians of the family's honour ensuring that daughters and other unmarried female members of the family were closely supervised to avoid tainting by male contacts and by gossip. Secondly, they tended to be the intermediaries in marriage transactions. Thirdly, they had the most active role within the community in keeping the religious rules and rituals and celebrating the seasonal festivities of Greek Orthodoxy. They whitewashed houses, decorated the epitaphios, organised the performance of rites, baked sweetmeats for the *panegyria* and so on. It was they who organised the household space symbolically, decorating the house with religious pictures and family photographs, particularly of weddings and baptisms. It was women, generally, who kept contact with relatives who had migrated and it was they who possessed practical knowledge of families and made reputations or marred them in the village community.

The dowry contract (even after it was legally abolished in 1979) specified the terms under which marriage was to be enacted in relation to property. Since the 1940s this entailed an increasing expectation that brides should provide the home, whereas men brought into marriage long-term resources such as income. Apart from the clear advantages this gave women with property in the marriage market it facilitated the quick neo-local settlement of the young couple. Its implications for the development of capitalism are various: the maintenance of low wages on the assumption that no rent was paid; lopsided economic development through investment in property; and the impetus given to consumerism. These are all evident in contemporary Greek-Cypriot life.

The form of the marriage transaction, with its stress on locality, shared values and religion and the transference of property, encouraged intermarriage within social groupings, particularly religious and cultural ones, and contributed to the lack of intermarriage between Greek-Cypriots and Turkish-Cypriots.

There have been a number of changes that need to be noted, although in respect to marriage as an economic transaction and the dowry they have not been significant.[2] Women's position in general, however, has changed. In the few studies in which the position of women and their general attitudes have been the subject of investigation, it appears that girls especially in the towns and from the more educated levels expect and are given much more freedom of movement (Mylonas *et al.* 1982). The increasing participation of women in the labour market (House 1980) and in secondary and higher education are important indicators of social change as well as having consequences for women's position within the household although not necessarily of a 'liberating' kind. A visitor to one of the major towns will quickly notice the existence of a youth sub-culture in clothing and style which is modelled on western Europe and America and includes, for example, boys and girls frequenting hamburger bars and ice-cream parlours. However, these aspects of modern life have not penetrated the most rural areas. On the other hand, frequent visits from relatives living abroad, particularly the London Cypriots, as well as imported television programmes, like 'Dallas' and 'Dynasty', have inevitably left their mark on local traditional values and lifestyles. There has been less change, not surprisingly perhaps, as regards sexual behaviour. The stress on female sexual purity and the prohibition of extra-marital contact remains, although more contact and friendship cannot be prevented between the sexes with women's greater incorporation in the economy and education.[3] Marriage partners are more likely to be chosen by the young people themselves with an expectation of approval by the parents. However, the dowry house is not only retained as an ideal but has become more conspicuous and competitive as economic affluence has grown. It is recognised as a 'social reality' even though there is evidence that many young people disapprove of it (Mylonas *et al.* 1982). Indeed, the state reinforces the dowry rule by providing government housing for women refugees intending to marry but not for men, in order not to disadvantage refugee women in the marriage market. Whatever the intentions of this provision, it serves to give continuing formal recognition and assent to the dowry system.

Motherhood was the most central of the roles that women were expected to play traditionally. However, knowledge about contraception was often absent and its availability was limited. In any case the church prohibited the use of contraceptives and they were generally regarded as sinful. The ideological valuation of motherhood remains in contemporary Cyprus despite the greater use of contraceptives and the rapid decline in the birth rate (House 1981). In a study of the village Lysi immediately prior to 1974 (Markides *et al.* 1978), the majority of first births arrived a year after marriage, a 'proof' of male virility and an assertion of women's 'natural' mothering role.

Until 1974 abortion was legally prohibited, although, in practice, women were able to obtain abortions where they could afford them. The law was amended after 1974 when soldiers violated many women during the Turkish invasion. Abortion was legalised on grounds of rape or other circumstances which would cause a serious undermining of the status of the pregnant woman or her family, where two doctors testified that a pregnant woman was endangered by pregnancy or childbirth, or if the baby risked physical or mental abnormality. It is telling that this dramatic reform, undertaken under the auspices of the ecclesiastical courts, should be instigated not by the fact of rape itself but by rape by Turkish soldiers and fears about the possibility of bearing the children of the 'enemy'. This national 'enemy' was by now conceptualised as the Turkish Army and, by default, the population it was supposedly defending on the island, the Turkish-Cypriots.

The constitution of 1960, when Cyprus was granted independence, established formal political equality between men and women. Despite this, the constitution reinforced the dependence of women on men for communal identification. It established that a married woman belongs to the community to which her husband belongs, and that a male or female child under the age of 21 who is not married belongs to the community to which his or her father belongs. If the father is unknown the child belongs to the community to which his or her mother belongs. The father was designated as the legal guardian of children under the age of 18. Only in cases where there was no father was the mother the legal guardian (Cyprus Social Research Centre 1978).

Women and the national liberation struggle

The form that the national liberation struggle took in Cyprus was contextually related to the form of nationalism that arose within the Greek-Cypriot population and was articulated most forcefully by right wing and chauvinist elements. The EOKA fighters themselves, however, were in the main young Cypriot men and women from both rural and urban backgrounds who were fired by the Enosis ideology. This had become, by this time, the dominant form of ethnic consciousness for all sectors of the Greek-Cypriot population (Anthias & Ayres 1983).

Given the small population of the island and the military presence of the British as well as the co-optation of Turkish-Cypriots by the British as auxiliary policemen and in the militia, EOKA could only be effective as an urban guerilla movement.

Women's role in EOKA has rarely been given prominence. For example, none of the accolades given to ex-EOKA fighters during the post-independence period were received by women. Only as mothers of fallen heroes (like Afxendiou and Pallikarides) were women publicly acclaimed. The important 'rear' activities of women (Yuval-Davis 1985) greatly contributed to EOKA's success, however.

Women played a distinct role in the EOKA movement in relation to men. Firstly, they acted as foils for EOKA fighters and would often accompany men, for whom the British had put out warrants, into the mountains to secret hide-outs (as their wives, fiancées or sisters). In the context of Cypriot values this jeopardised their sexual honour since the company of strange men was frowned upon. There was always the risk that they would be seen or that their fathers or brothers would find out. As they were sworn to total secrecy by the organisation, it was difficult for them to account for their actions. In addition there was always the possibility of sexual harassment, although it appears that this rarely occurred, but some liaisons and romances did develop as one might have expected.

Secondly, women did not carry weapons as such, although they often transported them. For example, after an attack on British soldiers, which usually took place in a crowded street they would receive the weapons used by the men. As searches for weapons were usually only made on men, this minimised the risk of arrest.

Thirdly, women were responsible for carrying information and acted as messengers, often carrying notes and letters which were small enough to be concealed in their underclothes. They also acted as correspondence clerks gathering mail and sorting it out, and some had polygraphic machines hidden in their houses for printing pamphlets which they distributed. This was a task done primarily by schoolgirls.

Fourthly, there were a number of women's units who would actually go out after dark and throw bombs or carry bombs to pass to men.

All these were clearly vital activities and indicate that the risks that women took were often as great as men. Nonetheless, women on the whole were regarded with less suspicion by the British. There were, however, instances of women being arrested and charged. In addition it is important to note that women's involvement had implications for their personal emancipation – many prior to this had barely talked to a man let alone struck up common links.[4]

In the public consciousness, however, the image of women that predominated during this period was one of 'mother of our young martyrs', as tragic, black-clothed women, willing to offer their most precious possession, their sons, for the motherland. Concrete rewards were given neither to women fighters nor to the mothers of heroes after the struggle ended, however, and most of these women retreated into anonymity.

Discourses round refugees – the centrality of women

Women in Cyprus traditionally occupy the domestic sphere, and the loss of their homes and villages after the war was therefore regarded as particularly tragic (Evdokas *et al*. 1976; Phatoura *et al*. 1981; Anthias 1987). The loss of a supportive kinship network, of the community that they had lived their day to day lives in since birth (residence is usually matrilocal) and finally of their dowry-house came as a great and lasting shock to most women.

Homelessness on a vast scale was the most pressing problem the Cypriot state had to face in the immediate aftermath of the war. Initially, the refugees camped in the open ground wherever they could and very soon refugee camps were set up partly with aid from international refugee funds. The massive displacement of the population and the loss of 70 per cent (Public Information Office 1983) of the productive potential, along with major ports and airports, led to mass unemployment.

Since refugees lost their land and homes as well as whatever other property they possessed, they are unable to provide their daughters with a dowry house on marriage. We have already indicated that the state provides a house for intending brides but not refugee bride-grooms, on the assumption that women bring a house into the marriage transaction. In the case particularly of refugee men, it means if they marry a 'foreigner' they will not have a home and therefore will have to move into rented accommodation. Given that incomes have taken into account that most people don't pay rent (to the benefit of employers), they will be disadvantaged.

In order to be able to afford 'something better' than the housing financed by the state, many women have entered paid employment often for the first time. The loss of land and property have been one of the factors that have led to greater incorporation of women into the labour market, within the light manufacturing or service sectors of the economy that have themselves witnessed a rapid expansion (House 1980).

Whilst in the Turkish-Cypriot sector the authorities attempt to wipe out any signs of pre-1974 Cyprus by renaming roads and villages with Turkish names and eliminating any remnants of Greek-Cypriot habitation, the reverse is true in the Greek-Cypriot sector (King & Ladbury 1982). Impermanency is reinforced through the careful maintenance of Turkish-Cypriot names and signs and a rhetoric of 'return'. This is clearly seen as important in the political goal of re-establishing an independent unified state structure for which the return of refugees to their homes and villages is central. The pursuit of a 'comfortable impermanency', as ex-President Kyprianou has called it, has left its marks in a number of ways, however. One of the most significant is the creation and perpetuation of the 'refugee' category, with the continual retelling of the story of loss and uprooting and the reification in the public consciousness of 'our villages' and 'our homes'. Women particularly are central in this, since the villages and homes are experienced as 'lost' in a more fundamental way for them. The few studies that have been done (Evdokas *et al*, 1976; Phatoura *et al*. 1981; Anthias 1985) have indicated the greater cost to women and the greater reliance on 'return' for overcoming their continuing difficulties.

This construction of a refugee category locked in impermanency has also functioned to create an artificial unity to the refugee population where class differences are as evident as within the population as a whole. This supposed social homogeneity within the category and the reinforcement of the division between refugee and non-refugee militates against class discourse as well as drawing attention from those refugees from the commercial entrepreneurial class who have been given favourable financial terms by the Cypriot state in order to encourage the restructuration of Cypriot class division and society along the old lines.

Despite the ideology of return, it is widely recognised that not all refugees will be able to return to their homes and villages, given the interests of Turkey and the Turkish-Cypriots. This serves to construct a real division between refugees from those regions that are most likely to return in the event of a political settlement (such as those from Famagusta) and the rest, thus replacing the dominance of the real division of class differences within the refugee population to one of regional difference. Yet the rhetoric of return remains as a political weapon purveyed by the media, the schools and to a lesser extent the political parties. This leads to a highly contradictory situation – on the one hand a sense of impermanency and thus insecurity for a large proportion of the population, and on the other hand knowledge that the real alternatives to their present situation are very limited.

The case of a particular category of women created by the war, the wives of missing persons, those 2000 or so Greek-Cypriots whose whereabouts are unknown, illustrates most poignantly the importance of women and the family ideologically. These, unlike refugee women (although many of them are refugee women also) have not been given special help by the state (Roussou 1986). Many are economically dependent on their relatives and have had to revert to the pre-adult status that single and divorced women are subjected to, expected to obey their fathers and to forgo male contacts. Local gossip often acts as an effective policing mechanism. The rights of widows of dead soldiers are denied them, as their husbands have not been formally declared dead. They have no rights over their husbands' property nor can they become legal guardians of their children. No provisions were introduced to ensure that these women had access to their husbands' property. The moral and social pressure not to institute divorce proceedings which would allow them to marry again is great. The church still objects to granting divorce in many cases and will do so only if the woman has already established another relationship and home with another man.

DEMOGRAPHIC POLICIES

Two of the declared demographic aims of the Cypriot state are to reverse the decline in the birth rate and to raise the labour force participation of women. It is recognised (House 1981) that the potential conflict between these two goals requires policy intervention. In addition there is a concern with emigration. As the third Emergency Action Plan, 1979–81, states: 'As regards population, the Plan aims at the formulation of a proper policy which will gradually lead to the reversal of the various adverse trends and developments in the past few years, particularly as regards emigration and the fall in the birth rate' (Statistics and Research Department, Cyprus 1979: 52). The crude birth rate has fallen from 30 per 1000 between 1946 and 1950 and 25 per 1000 between 1961 and 1965 to 18.5 per 1000 in 1976, representing a decline of 40 per cent over the whole period. By 1985 the rate had increased slightly to 19 per 1000 (Agathangelou 1987: 5). There is an inverse relationship between fertility and education as well as between the crude birth rate and labour-market participation and fertility and urban settlement (House 1981).

It appears unlikely, however, that there can be a reversal of trends towards greater educational attainment for women and urbanisation, both of which are negatively linked to fertility. The state in any case desires an increase in women's economic activity.

A number of measures have been taken to encourage larger families. First of all are those provisions which are exclusively for families with more than four or in some cases more than five, children. For example, there has been free medical treatment available to all members of families with more than four children since 1983. Fare subsidies on public transport are provided, government building-plots are offered at reduced prices and large families have priority in all government housing-schemes. In addition, the eldest son of a large family serves a truncated military service and income tax relief is given for children under 16 attending secondary school and to working mothers for each child looked after in an approved nursery or kindergarten. There has also been an increase in marriage and maternity allowances which have been gradually introduced with the revision of the social insurance law.

In addition to these measures to encourage fertility there have been attempts to improve nursery and day-care provision in order to

allow mothers to work. Sex equality measures are also being introduced to protect pregnant women from dismissal, and maternity
leave with pay is being improved.

Finally, the Technical Committee on Population in its final report
recommended the provision of a monthly family allowance per child
to be given to families with at least four children below 18 for the
third and older children (Chappa 1987).

As part of its demographic policy, the state makes substantial
attempts to prevent the loss of ethnic identity of the large number of
Cypriots who emigrated (Anthias 1981). The Cypriot state sends an
educational mission with teachers and other personnel to Britain, for
example, where the largest number of Cypriots abroad have settled.
Soon after the Turkish invasion (1977) a small government department was set up (Service of Overseas Cypriots), to strengthen the
unity between Cypriots abroad and Cyprus and maintain identity and
culture. In addition, in order to limit the exodus of Cypriots abroad,
temporary employment in other countries is arranged at times of high
unemployment for particular groups.

Various incentives for repatriation have been introduced (Chappa
1987), and there have been special attempts to persuade intellectuals
and professionals to return. But, given the absence of a university
and of a culture open to critical discourse, as well as problems of
graduate unemployment, such moves are doomed to failure.

CONCLUSION

Cyprus appears to be locked in a permanent state of impermanency.
The possibility of a solution on the basis of some form of a federal
state structure has repeatedly faltered (Anthias 1987). While this
stalemate exists, there is the danger of the resurfacing of nationalist
extremism. Until the indigenous political leaders and intellectuals on
both sides can provide a critique and an alternative to the received
wisdoms that often pass as the history of the last 30 years, little hope
exists of overcoming attitudes that stand as powerful obstacles to a
permanent peaceful solution. In the north, Denktash's position as
leader has not been seriously challenged and the presence of the
Turkish army discourages open debate on the Cyprus problem. There
is widespread discontent, however, in the north with the lack of
economic progress; the high level of unemployment; the uncertainty
that Turkish-Cypriot 'southerners' face; the conflict with settlers

brought in from Turkey to change the demographic balance of Cyprus; and the continued interference from Ankara. Only an internationally recognised negotiated solution can resolve these difficulties and this requires concessions on both sides.

Women have been affected by ethnic and national struggles and have been used in a number of ways in the 'national interest'. It is a challenge to both class organisations and to women to resist their co-optation in the nationalist cause and rework alliances with the equivalent forms on the Turkish-Cypriot side in the interests of their whole of the *Cypriot* nation.

NOTES

1. There are difficulties in gaining access to information in respect of the Turkish-Cypriot sector, as little published work is available in English, the author does not speak Turkish and, as a Greek-Cypriot, faces difficulties in entering the Turkish-Cypriot sector.

2. As Cypriot society has become more differentiated so have practices relating to marriage and the dowry, with differences between urban and rural areas and in relation to class. In the main, however, the dowry remains significant in marriage choice and the expectations relating to property transference have grown with increasing affluence.

3. To a large extent it has always been the case that women from the higher economic classes have been more 'Westernised' in respect to sexual relations and this remains the case today with women from the towns and professional groupings more likely to accept sexual relations outside marriage than other women.

4. This account is based on information gathered through interviewing a number of women who had been active in EOKA and I am grateful for their willingness to share their experiences with me.

BIBLIOGRAPHY

Agathangelou, A. (1987) 'Patterns and Determinants of Fertility in Cyprus', paper presented to National Workshop on 'Population and Human Resources Development', Nicosia, 13–15 April.

Aimilianides, A. (1938) *The Law Relating to Mixed Marriages* (Greek) (Nicosia: Kypriakai Spoudai).

Anthias, F. (1981) 'Ethnicity and Class amongst Greek-Cypriot Migrants',
Ph.D thesis, University of London.
Anthias, F. (1987) 'Cyprus', in C. Clarke and T. Payne (eds), *Politics,
Security and Development in Small States* (London: Allen & Unwin).
Anthias, F. (1985) 'The Refugee Issue and Social Change in Cypriot Society',
unpublished paper.
Anthias, F. & R. Ayres (1979) 'Nationalism and Socialism in Cyprus', CSE
Conference Papers, Conference of Socialist Economics.
Anthias, F. & R. Ayres (1983) 'Ethnicity and Class in Cyprus', *Race and
Class*, vol. 25, no. 1, 58–76.
Attalides, M. (ed.) (1977) *Cyprus Reviewed* (Nicosia: Social Research
Centre). Edinburgh.
Attalides, M. (1979) *Cyprus: Nationalism and International Politics* (Edin-
burgh: Press).
St Cassia, P. (1980) 'A Study of Peyia', D Phil. thesis, University of
Cambridge.
Chappa, I. (1987) 'Population Policy Issues in Cyprus – Past, Present and
Future', paper presented to national workshop on 'Population and Human
Resources Development', Nicosia, 13–15 April.
Coufoudakis, V. (ed.) (1976) *Essays on the Cyprus Conflict* (New York: Pella
Publishing).
Cyprus Social Research Centre (1978) *Cypriot Women, Rise and Downfall*
(Nicosia: Public Information Office).
Evdokas, T., L. Mylona, K. Paschalis, K. Olympios, S. Chimona, E. Kalava,
N. Theodorou & E. Demetriadou (1976) *Cyprus Refugees* (Greek)
(Nicosia: Social–Psychological Studies).
Hitchens, C. (1984) *Cyprus* (London: Quartet Books).
House, W.J. (1980) *Labour Market Segmentation and Sex Discrimination in
Cyprus* (Nicosia: Statistics and Research Department).
House, W.J. (1981) *Socio-economic Determinants of Fertility* (Nicosia:
Statistics and Research Department).
House, W.J. (1985) *Cypriot Women in the Labour Market* (Geneva: ILO).
King, R. & S. Ladbury (1982) 'The Cultural Reconstruction of Political
Reality in Greek and Turkish Cyprus since 1974', *Anthropological Quar-
terly*, vol. 55, no. 1, 1–16.
Kitromilides, P. (1977) 'From Co-existence to Confrontation: The Dynamics
of Ethnic Conflict in Cyprus', in M. Attalides (ed.) (1977).
Kyriakides, S. (1968) *Cyprus, Constitutionalism and Crisis Government*
(University of Pennsylvania Press).
Loizou, P. (1976) 'Changes in Property Transfer among Greek-Cypriot
Villagers', *Man* NS, vol. 10, 503–23.
Markides, K., E. Nikita & E.Rangou (1978) *LYSI: Social Change in a
Cypriot Village* (Nicosia: Social Reseach Centre).
Mylonas, I., K. Paschalis, E. Kalava, N. Patsalidou & A. Erotokritou (1982)
The Cypriot Woman (Greek) (Nicosia: Social–Psychological Studies
Group).
Phatoura, M. *et al.* (1981) *Cypriot Refugees* (Greek) (Thessalonika Uni-
versity).
Public Information Office (1983) *Cyprus – The Refugee Problem.*

Roussou, M. (1986) 'Women and Political Conflict in Cyprus', in R. Ridd and H. Calloway (eds), *Caught up in Conflict* (London: Macmillan).

Statistics and Research Department, Cyprus (1979) Third Emergency Action Plan.

Yuval-Davis, N. (1985) 'Front and Rear: the Sexual Division of Labour in the Israeli Army', *Feminist Studies*, vol. 11, no. 3, 649–76.

10 Women as the Family: the Foundation of a New Italy?
Lesley Caldwell

INTRODUCTION

This chapter argues that it is through understanding the legacy of the past, particularly the immediately preceding 20 years, that we can more clearly see how the Italian liberal democratic state has attended to women. It stresses the attempts to establish women as a separate constituency fundamental to the construction of a new Italian nation, a nation distinctively different from that aspired to by fascism. It argues that all women were to be legislated for and attended to as part of the progressive stamp of the new republic; at the same time they were, in their traditional familial role, and above all as mothers, to be enlisted in the building of this new nation. By reference to statements from the 1943–8 period, it aims to show some of the problems involved in the new state, fundamentally adhering to traditional understandings of women's needs, obligations, rights and duties, while at the same time endorsing aspirations for progressive legislative reforms in their favour.

WOMEN AND THE STATE IN POST-SECOND WORLD WAR ITALY

The period following the arrest of Mussolini (July 1943) and the collapse of the fascist regime was one of massive political and social upheaval. Italy was devastated by the continuation of the world war raging in Europe generally and in the national territory in particular. In 1946 a referendum established the republic and dissolved the monarchy; women were given the vote in that year. Economic and social reconstruction involved the establishment of a new political machinery that would direct a different form of state. An interim government, 1946–8, distinguished by two different coalitions, was made responsible for drawing up the constitution.

In the period 1943–8 there were inevitably whole areas of continuity with fascism. These included the form of personnel, of laws, of some state institutions and of the re-endorsement of the fascist state's agreements with the Vatican. This continuity is of particular interest in matters of women and the family. Moreover, it suggests that the importance of the ideological and cultural dimensions of the transformation were more porblematic than the dismantling of the more straightforwardly repressive aspects of fascism. The continuities, as Pavons (1974: 140) insists, built on the continuities of a particular class domination and socio-economic structure. They are also the result of the political choices followed through in the 1943–7 period and the continuities represented by the line of heads of government in which there was no rupture. These choices were not only the result of the estimation and strategies of the political parties involved but also of the pressures from the Allies for reconstruction in a particular way.

The historical role of Catholicism is also central in understanding developments in the Italian national state from 1946 onwards. The late unification of Italy (1861) was effected against the claims of organised Catholicism and one way the church attempted to counter the power of the centralised state was through the development of cultural, educational, financial and welfare networks.

The area of welfare assistance is especially relevant here, since much discussion of state support involves the provision of services that are seen as supplementing and extending the needs attended to families, especially by mothers. The state law of 1890 that grouped welfare institutions under state control in practice often left that control to the church. This is important because the way the church and certain apparatuses of the state have combined and divided areas of responsibility which in other countries have been more tightly brought under state control is an important aspect of the Italian situation after 1948, where, until the 1970s, church-supported institutions have supplemented and provided what the state does/did not in care and provision for children, the old, the sick and so on.

The 20 years of fascism relates both to the church (although this cannot be discussed here) and to the position of women. In Italy it is above all fascism that introduced legislation regarding social assistance and insisted on the obligation of the state to provide for the family (Saraceno 1981). This was linked to a concern with the forging

of a strong and healthy Italian nation through an overt set of policies
that aimed at population increase. These policies were especially,
though not exclusively, directed at women as mothers; they included
encouragement to get married and to produce large families.[1] The
fascists also introduced advanced legislation relating to working
mothers; they restructured but did not substantially alter the family
law that had been in operation since 1865; they introduced penalties
for abortion and forbade the spread of information on contraception.
Perhaps of even greater importance for the discussion here, they
operated an extended propaganda campaign on the importance of
women's place in the family and the personal and national importance of motherhood. This represents a generalisable trend in the
twentieth-century state towards responsibility for regulation of
increasingly large areas of the apparently personal and private life.
L'ONMI, *Opera Nazionale Maternita Infanzia*, was the first state
organisation with national responsibility for the needs of mothers and
children. Founded in 1925, it lasted till 1975. It is the institution of
prime importance here.

There was continuity in laws regarding the protection of
motherhood and infancy; the norms governing welfare for illegitimate and abandoned children or foundlings; the health law; the
family law (revised 1975); the juvenile court and its organisation; the
forms of regulation of 'criminal' minors; the penal code. The latter
has still not received complete revision, although some of its Articles
have been revoked. Of specific relevance here are the Articles
referring to abortion, to the sale and advertisement of contraceptives
and the differential criminal status of adultery. The modes by which
women are separately attended to in these laws reproduce the
emphases of fascism but they also further legitimise church positions.
The heritage left by the fascist state, the powerful position of the
Catholic Church and the growing state concern for families and for
mothers reveals a powerful interlocking set of mechanisms in postwar
Italy. Official state documents like the constitution, in existence
alongside discriminatory laws, construct and legitimise particular
accounts of women and of relations between mother and child. These
make demands for freedom from traditional female roles for women
more difficult to enact. Arguably it was only in the 1970s that a
significant shift occurred in the legal position of women as bearers of
reproductive capacities which do not automatically negate their other
rights as Italian citizens.

In Italy the Catholic Church has reinforced the tendency to regard women as biological reproducers and nurturers and to regard them highly. There are clearly parallels between fascist rhetoric on motherhood and the church's stress on women as mothers first and foremost. When similar views about women are reproduced in official state accounts their importance is further extended by the association with church accounts. This highlights the difficulty of offering alternative accounts or positions when the preceding years had been dominated with a concern with women as reproducers and as builders of the nation only in so far as they *were* reproducers. The new Italian state, through official texts and other statements, insists that it is distancing itself from the fascist regime in that it sees women as equal partners in the construction of a new nation. However, in certain of its statements (say, Article 2 the constitution), it guarantees female equality, but in other of the Articles of the constitution it formally disavows this equality (Article 37). In its more general claims and appeals to all women it inveighs against the position offered to woman under fascism, but continues to endorse laws formulated under the fascist regime. The new state inevitably utilises and draws upon accounts of what it is to be a woman, and an Italian woman, that substantially reproduce those of fascism.

Examination of the debates surrounding the constitution reveals an inability and a refusal to go beyond cultural assumptions about women as biological reproducers. This works alongside the Catholic account of the family, women's primary position in it and the ordering of more general civil rights on that basis. And it is this that contributes to the long delays in reforming whole areas of the law that are seen to touch women in their familial obligations first and foremost. The legislators for the new nation, for all their insistence on the imperative need to take their distance from fascism, are caught in an extremely contradictory view of women and their proper and just place in a new and progressive democracy. For, as fascism demonstrated in a more clear cut way, the emphasis on reproduction entails other implications for the social position of women, implications that in hierarchically ordering their capacities and legislation either protectively or repressively about them may be used to justify other sets of sanctioned but potentially oppressive practices. The uncritical identification of Italian women as mothers, common to fascism and the Catholic Church, forms the basis of discussion in the establishment of the liberal democratic republic. The position offered to women is one that seeks to endorse their rights as citizens while insisting that motherhood is their major contribution to the building of a new collectivity, a nation united. A generalised rhetoric appeal to all women is the norm. Its basis is that of biological sex and the capacity to reproduce, and it is completely taken for granted. But the meanings associated with this are only established with reference to the structuring conditions of women's lives and there is a vast step from the attribution of a potential to the concrete conditions in which actual women may, can and do exercise three capacities. Here age, class situation, marital status and geographical location are important, and it is by reference to specific laws that ways of legislating for women as wives, as mothers, as older women and as workers may be distinguished.

But the discussions about the place women are offered or called upon to occupy in the new Italian nation make their appeal to a presumed unity whose basis is the cultural traditions that link the biological and the social. It is clear that there is a disjunction between the number of central structuring issues glossed over by the appeal to all women and the omnipresence of these other appeals. Public rhetorics of difference, the claims through which the demonstrable gap between the former shamed regime and the present–future one which the strengths of democracy are paramount, were an extremely important target. How 'women' feature in statements of the period gives important indicators on how they are discursively constituted in the new Italy and the kinds of roles assigned to them.

At the General Sitting of the Constituent Assembly on International Women's Day, 8 March 1947, it is one of the 22 women representatives who confirms the identification of women and the family. She uses it to draw out two important emphases: the first is the idea of the Italian nation as a family, that is attended to by women; and the second the union of national and Christian (i.e. Catholic) ideas in support of this:

> We do not forget, and we never shall forget, that our first task, and the highest and most social one, is the family; that motherhood is our privilege and because of that, we have claimed, are claiming, from the new constitution those new legal dispositions, like the family wage, like limits of women's work, that allow us to fully attend to our family function:
>
> Moreover, today, we feel that a much broader family demands our sacrifices and dedication; that all the Italian people are our family and that we must work to bring the spirit of the family into this social family. This is precisely the Christian spirit. (Session of the Assembled Constituents, 8 March 1947)

In the next section of this chapter I briefly present three contemporary sets of statements about women and the family. These are:

(1) the discussions in the Constituent Assembly on the Constitution;
(2) statements from the Italian Communist Party (PCI);
(3) statements from the Union of Italian Women (UDI).

Each of these occupies a very different terrain, comprises different aims and objects and assumes a radically different weight institutionally and politically. My aim in bringing them together is to testify to the ways and forms through which the variety of discourses about women and the family were commonly articulated in a vital period for postwar Italy. I suggest that the reliance on a set of understandings of the elision between women and the family and women and mothers is common to all three sets, that the tenacity of these accounts owes much to the strength of Catholicism and the legacy of facism, and that the task of legislating a different place for women is ultimately dependent on a biologism whose cultural effects act to constrain the official legal position of Italian women despite the activities of the women's emancipation movement and the workers' movements for much of the postwar period. The directions politically set in place during this time, the legal formulations role for Italian women as their special responsibility and expectation combine to establish some of the structuring conditions through which other massive postwar changes, e.g. emigration, have had their effects and are to be understood.

Aspirations towards formal equality conceal a multitude of problems in attempting a separate appeal to women as *first* women and *then* Italian citizens. The nationalist appeal gains strength through identification with other, taken-for-granted sources of emotional security and privilege.

THE CONSTITUENT ASSEMBLY

Elections for the Constituent Assembly, one of whose major tasks would be to draw up the constitution of the republic, were held in 1946. In these elections Christian democrats gained 35.2 per cent of the vote and the PCI–PSI combined, 39.6 per cent proportion to their overall elected numbers. Of the 20 women who had been elected to the Assembly four took part in the three sub-commissions set up to hammer out a form of wording for certain Articles, two communists, a socialist, and a Christian democrat.

This section refers to the substance of the discussions in the First and Third Sub-Commissions, respectively concerned with legal definitions of the family and marriage, and with state concern for the economic and social problems of the family. These Commissions met through the latter half of 1946, and their decisions were incorporated in Articles 3, 29, 31, 37 of the Constitution.[2] But it is the bases and presuppositions of these meetings that is of interest here. The final wording of the constitution establishes a series of norms that confirm a woman's place as mother as 'essential'. This directs many of the other issues, especially those with more direct policy implications, and serves to impede the other struggles for women's rights before the law in the subsequent period.

These meetings form a core of debates about how the family is to be understood and its institutional position guaranteed. The extent to which the family is seen as known and relatively unproblematic appears to depend on an absolute insistence on the role of women as mothers within it. It is not just that women are mothers first and foremost, it is that women *as* mothers may be seen as the guarantors of the family whether its timelessness and eternal aspects are being stressed or whether it is the family as an historically specific institution that is emphasised. There is little disagreement about the claims of motherhood and about women's primary familial location even when it is women workers that are the ostensible focus, or when equal treatment is being argued in conjunction with the idea that men and women have a different mission:

> The special and essential mission of woman is motherhood. This is a concept that must always be kept in the forefront. When there is concern for the working woman this is a concern above all for the fact of motherhood, for the tutelage of her condition before, during and after birth. What must be guaranteed to the working woman is being able to deal adequately with those special needs that surround maternity. (Terracini, in full session of the Assembled Constituents, 1947 p. 206)

This condensation of women's identity within the family is accompanied by a failure to recognise the complexity of state regulation of motherhood. For example, in the discussion on provision for mothers and for youth (Sessions of the Prima Sottocommissione, 7 November

1946 p. 372) the discussion never touches maternity; the appropriate forms of provision for the young are discussed but the one central provision concerning support for maternity is agreed in the First Commission without any discussion of its implications. Or in the Third Sub-Commission the discussion on the social function of motherhood, introduced by Teresa Noce (PCI) consistently adhered to the idea of the mother as the family despite discussion of irregular familial arrangements, such as unmarried mothers:

> Protection for mothers means protection for society at its roots because around the mother, the family is established and through the mother, society's future is guaranteed. There is a need for insurance but also for welfare. Further, confirming the principle of the protection of the mother means attending to *all* children, including illegitimate ones. (Merlin, in the Session of the Prima Sottocommissione. 1946 p. 34)

Both this point and the discussion in the First Commission on state financial support for the family came up against Catholic belief about normal families and conservative restrictions on state support for the unworthy or the immoral, but the general point was unanimously accepted.

Togliatti (PCI) argues that women work both outside and inside the family, without prioritising one or the other, but still says that 'generally' women as mothers *are* the family. Moro (DC), concerned that women's entry into public life may lead to less weight being given to their familial roles, wants the constitution not only to guarantee certain things about the family but to structure and constrain women so as to ensure a continuation of their familial role and the primacy of their biological potential. (Sessions of the Prima Sottocommissione, 1946 p. 207).

Although the very themes that distinguish these debates testify to the framework of Catholic understandings that provide the discursive parameters here, there is little clear agreement about them, or about the policy implications that derive from them. However, the unanimity about women as the family is clear and indicates their central place in ensuring a healthy Italian nation.

The themes of these debates indicate the recognition that the modern state must assume responsibility and concern for areas that had been largely unattended to. Concern for the individual and for the private space of the family and its rights is also consistently put forward. The links between family, state and individual are seen as problematic and to be legislated in conformity with other emphases, the link between family and nation previously mentioned and the issue of whether the family is a natural association (a Catholic formulation).

To give two examples of the latter:

> There can be no doubts about the fact that the family is a natural society. (Sessions of the Prima Sottocommissione, 5 November 1946 p. 388; Sitting (11))

> Saying that the family is recognised by the state in so far as it is a natural society means allowing the possibility of that recognition even for families that are constituted outside the marital bond, families, that is, that are deprived of the crism of legality and the religious sacrament. In this sense concubinage would be recognised by the state. (ibid, 339)

The small degree of agreement on these issues is not surprising given the vast range of issues gathered under the rubric of the family: for example, the rights of and between married couples in relation to their children and the conditions in which state intervention can be countenanced; the relentless adherence to the metaphor of the health of the country as residing in the healthy family with indissolubility the only ultimate guarantee of this individual as well as national territorial stability; the family as bearer of the moral standards of a new society; the recognition that without certain external support, financial or otherwise, the family cannot fulfil its functions.

Throughout these debates the merging of the identity of woman with the family and with the new Italy is assumed. This acts to single women out as indispensible contributors to the forging of the new nation. Within the discussion of rights it also aims to extend a place to women as citizens, a place symbolised by the vote. But the retention of inegalitarian laws alongside the stress on the primacy of the family as women's place creates a set of difficult and restrictive norms from which to pursue women's parity with men.

THE ITALIAN COMMUNIST PARTY (PCI)

The Italian Communist Party had been founded in 1921 and under fascism existed underground or outside Italy. Party members were active organisers in the Resistance, participated in the committees of national liberation in the period after 1943, and collaborated in successive governments until their expulsion in May 1947, an expulsion which was tied to continued US support for reconstruction. In the PCI after 1944 its leader, Togliatti, saw reconstruction in terms of the establishment of a pluralist party system and the abandonment of working class opposition, in favour of collaboration with all democratic forces in the construction of a new 'demographic regime'. The continuity of PCI policy on this issue is fairly generally attested (Blackmer 1977; Napolitano 1977; Sassoon 1977). But it is its position on the family and its understanding of the 'woman question' that is of interest here.

The PCI's development of the 'woman question' in the postwar period is organised on an axis where poles are the family and its capacity for change on the one hand, and women's rights to waged work on the other. Theoretically and politically, the party combines the emphases of the international communist movement with the strength of cultural traditions that echo those of Catholicism.

Togliatti, leader of the PCI from his return from Moscow (1944) to his death in 1964, identified women as one of the major groups who would contribute to the reconstruction of Italy. Their centrality was a position shared neither by all party members nor all cadres, men or women. Togliatti's account encloses the specificity of the woman question in a set of Marxist categories that tie women's oppression to class oppression and to the need for a complete transformation of all existing social relations. But an elaboration of the woman question that engaged with its more problematic aspects is absent from PCI accounts. The importance of the family both for the Italian nation and for the health of all its citizens is continually insisted upon and the recourse to very traditional images of motherhood and femininity remain the central stamp of these accounts.

Unlike the Catholics, the communists do not dispute the supposed disruption of the bases of family life implied as following from women's waged work. They argue its necessity for the emancipatory process, but their position does not depend on a different evaluation of women's 'natural' role nor any challenge to their primary familial location. 'Today the family presents itself more than ever before as the original nucleus on which the citizens and the state must depend for the social and moral renewal of Italy (Rinascita 1 September 1946).

This article by Jotti sets out some of the considerations on the family that shape PCI statements in the period under study and well beyond. On the basis of the disruption and chaos occasioned by fascism, wartime conditions and the occupation, the family, given its traditional primacy in Italian life, is regarded as the obvious place from which to begin a reconstruction of the unity and solidarity that will be required to forge the nation anew: 'The state recognizes and attends to the family as the foundation of the material and moral prosperity of the nation' (Jotti 1946).

In conjunction with the party's emphasis on the moral position of the family it is the links between family, state and nation that provide the major orientation for the PCI's accounts for legislative reform. The latter sought to equalise the status of husbands and wives, to remove the anti-democratic features endorsed by fascism and to give the family those marks of serenity and dignity that would enable women to see marriage in a completely different way; through legal reform the family would become 'a font of joy and an aid for the development of the real personality of the wife':

> The woman acquires an independence (through right to work and other legal rights) that allows her to see marriage not as an expedient forced upon her as the only means of solving a difficult economic situation but as the satisfaction of a deep natural, moral and social need, as the means of her development and the crowning glory of her personality. (Jotti 1946)

In this account the links between marriage, the family and women's particular relation to it are as unproblematically tied together for the party as they are for the church. Despite the importance of the discourse of work for the communists they retain a conception of women's essential 'womanliness' that is not only linked to her familial locations but crucially dependent on it.

The PCI argues for state regulation through the introduction of welfare measures that will complement the necessary and desired work of women and will also provide the facilities for a different set of possibilities both in the family and in the more general relation between family and society. From the 1940s on, then, the PCI consistently support demands for state assistance and for the development of a network of health, education and social services that will provide an infrastructure of support enabling the Italian family to flourish and to provide the maximum possibilities for its members and for society.

Here the PCI may be seen as representing one wing of the modernising voices; their explicit commitment is to the need for state support and state intervention and an insistence that the modern family does not manage alone. But, in recognising the comprehensive and contradictory demands placed on the modern family, the PCI insists that it does not wish to deny the differences between men and women, or the privacy of the family; rather, its aim is to offer a different position to women in the family and a new position for the family in society, which, far from destroying the family, will safeguard and strengthen it.

UNIONE DONNE ITALIANE (UDI)

The Union of Italian Women (UDI) dates from September 1944. The initiative grew out of the groups for the defence of women that had grown up in the north towards the end of 1943 and groups in the centre and in Naples associated with the circulation of a clandestine news-sheet, *No. 1 Donne*.

Initial hopes for a united organisation were unsuccessful and Catholic women remained apart in their own separate organisation. The history of UDI, as it relates to a politics of and for women conducted within a commitment to socialist perspectives, is an important one both from the point of view of its gains and its losses. Its position is characterised particularly by a twofold orientation: firstly, an acknowledgement of the strength of Catholicism and a wish to avoid any challenge to it; and secondly, an account that sees the masses of Italian women trapped in traditional understandings, a situation encouraged and exaggerated by facism.

Within these perspectives UDI was committed to the link between family and nation and, in line with its strong links with the PCI, the link between the renewal of Italian society and women's emancipation. It aimed to provide a means for all Italian women to participate in the political and social life of the country.

As Mafai (1979: 37) points out, women in the Resistance are afterwards mobilised on two fronts. One of these was to provide assistance of various kinds to male combatants as well as providing support for families, children and so on. Although this was a traditional form of women's activity (both organised and unorganised), it was nonetheless important. The other, participation in military campaigns etc., was distinctively different. Both of these fronts need to be recognised and understood, as does the situation of the many women who remained outside either of them. The armed struggle was a mode of participation for both men and women for a far briefer time, but with this proviso: the major orientation in the post-liberation period was consistently towards traditional female tasks, combined with a commitment to full civil rights for women and the attempts to mobilise women workers.

The First Congress in October 1945 stressed the conquest of political rights and full participation for women in the life of the country; it especially stressed the right to work, demanded equal pay for equal work, improved working conditions, the provision of nurseries and the provision of training schools such as those that existed for men. It also stressed the need to guarantee women at home 'an adequate protection in law'. The conference argued for the education of women through the establishment of classes at work, evening classes, travelling libraries etc., all designed to begin to counteract the position of degradation and ignorance encouraged by fascism. These aims, together with the demand for legal reforms to ensure the removal of gross inequalities within families and the provision of welfare services, conform to traditional ways of effecting change in the practice of women's organisations.

In the sphere of response to the devastation of war, hunger and starvation, there is also the view of the family as an 'irreplaceable and fundamental nucleus', and a stress on the role of mother within it. This is not to underestimate the task in hand at that time but at this time one looks in vain to the specifically directed women's organisation for a recognition of some of the problems that pertain to the elision of women and the family.

> In the pursuit of a politics for the new Republic it is again the family that is given pride of place, it is the family on which the new Nation depends, and it is the family that is seen as the thing to safeguard. The inappropriateness of putting other views and the directions taken then establish forms of accommodation that endure until the seventies. One looks in vain for the public voice of opposition.
>
> When you have the will, there's time for everything; this is what those women who don't shut themselves egotistically in their own homes know. They understand that being mothers means that through their love for their own children they arrive at a love for all babies. In this way they recognise the imperative of working to construct a future of peace and well-being for all. (I Camino, 1945–6)

CONCLUSION

In this chapter I have suggested that the Italian Republic was concerned constitutionally to offer women an equality they had never had before. This had the support of the Communist Party and the Socialist Women's Organisation. How this was argued and presented reveals a basic set of assumptions that remain unchallenged in the period and for some considerable time after. In itself this may not have been so significant but for the generalised insistence on the appeal for distance and separation from the former regime.

The project of legislating and prescribing a different way of regulating women when the terms in which this is presented are almost identical, is one that is extremely daunting. There is considerable hesitation and distaste for the extremes of fascist demographic propaganda, but not sustained challenge to its assumptions. The constitutional aspirations co-exist perfectly well alongside the extensive commitment to Catholic concepts and alongside the laws that prescribe profoundly unequal parental and marital relations.

Motherhood in Italy has been idealised certainly, but the tenacity with which it was invoked in the period of reconstruction and the durability of these accounts was materially and legally supported by the new Italian state above all in defining a specific space for women in the construction of the new, and distinctively different, Italy. I have pointed to the difficulties for those postwar organisations committed to a politics of and for women by the initial inability to look beyond women's biological capacity.

NOTES

1. For an account of the fascist period, see L. Caldwell, 'Reproducers of the Nation', in D. Forgacs (ed.) *Rethinking Italian Fascism* (London: Lawrence & Wishart, 1986).
2. Article 3.
   All citizens are invested with equal social status and are equal before the law, without distinction as to sex, race, language, religion, political opinions, personal or social conditions.
   Article 29.
   The state recognises the family as a natural association founded on marriage.

Marriage is based on the moral and legal equality of husband and wife within the limits laid down by the law for ensuring family unity.
Article 31.
The republic facilitates, by means of economic and other provisions, the formation of the family and the fulfilment of the tasks connected therewith, with particular consideration for large families.

It safeguards maternity, infancy and youth, promoting and encouraging institutions necessary for such purposes.
Article 37.
Female labour enjoys equal rights and the same wages for the same work as male labour. Conditions of work must make it possible for them to fulfil their essential family duties and provide for the adequate protection of mothers and children.

The republic prescribes special measures for safeguarding juvenile labour and guarantees equal pay for equal work.

BIBLIOGRAPHY

Ballastrero, M.V. (1979) *Dalla tutela alla parita* (Bologna: Il Mulino).

Blackmer, D. (1977) 'Continuity and Change in Postwar Italian Communism', in D. Blackmer & S. Tarrow (eds) (1977).

Blackmer, D. & S. Tarrow (eds) (1977) *Communism in Italy and France* (Princeton University Press).

Caldwell, L. (1986) 'Reproducers of the Nation', in D. Forgacs (ed.) *Rethinking Italian Fascism* (London: Lawrence & Wishart).

Camino, Il in 'Internal Document of UDI' (Union of Italian Women), 1945.

Candeloro, G. (1953) *Il movimento cattolico in Italia* (Rome: Riuniti).

Jotti, N. (1946) 'La famiglia e lo stato', *Rinascita*, 1 September.

Mafai, M. (1979) *L'apprendistato della politica* (Rome: Editori Riuniti).

Michetti, M., M. Repetto and L. Viviani (1984) *UDI: Laboratorio di politica delle donne* (Rome: Cooperative libera stampa).

Napolitano, G. (1977) *The Italian Road to Socialism* (London: Journeyman Press).

Pavone, C. (1974) 'La continuita dello stato Instituzioni e uomini', in AAVV *Italia 1945–1948. Le origini della repubblica* (Turin: Giappicheli).

Poggi, G. (1972) 'The Church in Italian Politics 1945–1956', in S.J. Woolf (ed.) (1972).

Saraceno, C. 'Percorsi di vita femminile nella classe operaia. Tra famiglia e lavora durante il fascismo', *Memoria*, vol. 2 (October) 64–75.

Sassoon, D. (1977) 'The Ideology and Strategy of the Postwar Italian Communist Party', doctoral dissertation, London University.

Woolf, S.J. (ed.) (1972) *The Rebirth of Italy 1943–50* (London: Longman).

Official documents

Sessions of the Assembled Costituente, 1947. Full.
Sessions of the Prima Sottocommissione, 26 July–19 December 1946.
Sessions of the Terza Sottocommissione, 26 July–26 October 1946.

Index